CORPOLOGY DECODED

SANGEETA MUKHERJEE

BLUEROSE PUBLISHERS
U.K.

Copyright © Sangeeta Mukherjee 2025

All rights reserved by author. No part of this publication may be reproduced, stored in a retrieval system or transmitted in any form or by any means, electronic, mechanical, photocopying, recording or otherwise, without the prior permission of the author. Although every precaution has been taken to verify the accuracy of the information contained herein, the publisher assumes no responsibility for any errors or omissions. No liability is assumed for damages that may result from the use of information contained within.

BlueRose Publishers takes no responsibility for any damages, losses, or liabilities that may arise from the use or misuse of the information, products, or services provided in this publication.

For permissions requests or inquiries regarding this publication, please contact:

BLUEROSE PUBLISHERS
www.BlueRoseONE.com
info@bluerosepublishers.com
+4407342408967

ISBN: 978-93-7139-960-9

Cover design: Daksh
Typesetting: Tanya Raj Upadhyay

First Edition: June 2025

With Love and Gratitude

To my parents,

Your belief in me has been my compass.

Mom, you once hoped I would become a college professor, shaping minds in a classroom. That didn't quite happen (life had other plans).

But with this little book, I hope I have done something in the spirit of your dream, nudging young minds gently toward growth, courage, and clarity.

To my mentors, teachers, coaches, and trainers,

You lit lamps on foggy days and offered wisdom when I needed it most.

Thank you for seeing potential where I saw only questions.

To the good bosses, thank you for your trust and guidance.

To the not-so-good bosses, thank you for teaching me patience, grit, and the art of silent eye rolls.

Both shaped me.

To my peers and friends, your laughter, real talk, and timely reminders ("You've got this") carried me forward more times than you know.

This book is a quiet prayer, a thank-you letter, and a mirror for those just starting out.

May it make them feel a little more prepared, a little less alone, and a lot more powerful.

With all my heart,

Sangeeta Mukherjee

Preface

When I stepped into the corporate world 17 years ago, I was full of hope, ambition, and the belief that hard work, punctuality, and a well-crafted résumé would be enough to succeed. Like many freshers, I was eager to learn, ready to prove myself, and excited about the journey ahead.

What I didn't quite see coming was the subtle undercurrent that flows quietly beneath everyday work life - the unspoken norms, the quiet expectations, the gentle sway of office politics, and the delicate art of perception. These aren't usually found in job descriptions or training manuals, but they play a big role in how things move at work. And while people don't always talk about them openly, they are very real, and they shape a lot of our experiences.

I still remember one of my earliest lessons. During a casual coffee chat, I shared an idea with a colleague, only to hear that same idea was presented in our team meeting moments later, without any mention of my name. It stung deeply and taught me early on how credit and recognition can shift quietly in the corporate world. That moment was my first glimpse into the "real" corporate playbook.

Over the years, I stumbled, observed, adapted, and grew. From a quiet note-taker, I gradually became a confident leader, learning how to speak up, build alliances, and navigate politics without compromising my values. Most importantly, I discovered that doing good work is essential, but being visible for that work is equally critical. I am still learning to navigate through thick and thin, but trust me, the journey is quite endearing.

Corporate life has been one of my greatest teachers. Though overwhelming at first, it has shaped me into the person I am today, more resilient, strategic, and self-aware. It taught me that the workplace is not just about tasks but also about relationships, influence, and integrity.

This book, *Corpology Decoded*, is my humble attempt to share the lessons I have learnt, those hidden truths and unwritten rules of the corporate world that no textbook covers. This book is for anyone stepping into this complex, exciting, and sometimes confusing environment.

Just in case you are wondering, why the name, Corpology Decoded? Well, here's the thing: what we study in books is just the tip of the iceberg. We read about leadership, emotional intelligence, and organizational behaviour, all of which are important, no doubt. But the real corporate world? It speaks a whole different language. It's a world with its own set of unspoken instructions, hidden cues, and subtle dynamics, things no textbook really prepares you for. I call it Corpology because corporate life almost feels like its own subject, one that needs decoding. And that's exactly what this book is here to do, to help you make sense of what's often left unsaid but deeply shapes your journey.

You will not find yourself alone when reading this book. We have a special mentor for you. Growing up, I was enchanted by the tales of Akbar and Birbal. For those unfamiliar, Emperor Akbar was a wise and visionary ruler in 16th-century India, and Birbal was his trusted advisor known for his sharp wit, intelligence, and fairness. Together, they navigated the challenges of the royal court with humour, wisdom, and kindness.

These stories were more than just entertaining; they were life lessons. Birbal's calm, clever approach to solving problems inspired me throughout my corporate journey. I often found myself asking, *"what would Birbal do?"* when facing challenging situations at work.

The modern office, in many ways, feels like a royal court, filled with complex relationships, power dynamics, and moments requiring both grace and grit. Birbal's timeless wisdom, characterized by integrity, humour, and strategic kindness, offers a unique lens through which we can understand and navigate today's workplace.

In *Corpology Decoded*, you will find Birbal's spirit woven throughout. This book offers real-life stories, reflection prompts, and practical advice on:

- Handling rejection with dignity
- Understanding and rising above office politics
- Recognizing why perception often matters more than performance
- Building an authentic personal brand
- Navigating the patience and politics of promotions
- Decoding corporate lingo in an approachable way

Whether you are a fresher or finding your foothold, I hope this book becomes a trusted companion, helping you feel seen, understood, and equipped to thrive.

Corpology Decoded isn't about shortcuts but about insight, learning to be strategic without losing authenticity, speaking up without losing kindness, and knowing when to push and when to pause.

Your corporate journey is not just about climbing a ladder; It's about asking:

Where does the ladder lead?

Who is holding it?

And is it even leaning against the right wall?

Welcome to *Corpology Decoded*. Let's decode the corporate world, one story at a time.

Table of Content

THE POWER OF 'NO' 1
    HOW TO HANDLE REJECTION 1
OFFICE POLITICS 11
    NAVIGATING THE UNSEEN GAME 11
PERCEPTION BUILDING 23
    YOUR IMAGE MATTERS 23
RECOGNITION VS. DILIGENCE 36
    THE UNSUNG HEROES PATH 36
WORK ETHICS AND INTEGRITY 47
    THE CORNERSTONES OF SUCCESS 47
BUILDING YOUR PERSONAL BRAND 57
    BE MEMORABLE 57
DOING THE RIGHT THINGS 67
    VERSUS. DOING THINGS RIGHT 67
PATIENCE AND PROMOTIONS 77
    THE LONG GAME 77
CORPORATE CULTURE 87
    ADAPTING AND THRIVING 87
YOUR CREDIBILITY SPEAKS 97
    LET YOUR ACTIONS DEFINE YOU 97

FREQUENTLY USED CORPORATE JARGONS 109

    SPEAK THE LINGO - CRACKING THE CORPORATE CODE 109

ACKNOWLEDGEMENTS & REFERENCES 114

AUTHOR'S LETTER FOR YOU! 116

CHAPTER 1

THE POWER OF 'NO'
HOW TO HANDLE REJECTION

A 3-year-old boy was persistent about getting a balloon he saw flying high, but his mother said, 'No.' That kid felt bad, kept nagging, cried, showed a temper tantrum by yelling, but the mother was adamant with her 'No.' Probably, that was the first time a 3-year-old felt rejected. Hmm, it started too early.

A teenager was awestruck by watching a racing bike on television and asked his father to get him the same bike for his next birthday. His father nodded and said, *"You are too young to ride a racing bike. Maybe once you grow up, you can surely get one."* Perhaps the father was polite enough with a subtle 'No'. Without uttering a single word, the teenage boy marched into his room and slammed the door. He must have felt disheartened, right?

When dining with parents, a 19-year-old girl shared her ambitions to pursue higher studies abroad. Her parents looked at each other, laughed, and reminded her that she cannot even cook for herself, therefore, would not be able to manage abroad. Do you think that night the girl was able to sleep?

Let's talk about something no one likes but everyone faces,

REJECTION

Whether it's your brilliant idea getting shot down, your request for a promotion being ignored, or your project proposal being shelved, hearing 'No' can itch. It's easy to feel like you are not good enough or that your efforts don't matter. But here's the truth: rejection is not about you, it's about the situation. And guess what? It's one of the best teachers you will ever have.

Think about it. When was the last time you heard a 'No'? Was it your manager when you pitched a new idea, or a client who didn't like your proposal? How did it feel? Disappointing, right? But here's the thing: every 'No' is an opportunity in disguise. It's a chance to learn, grow, and come back stronger. A 'No' holds a lot of power.

Imagine you are in a meeting, and you have spent weeks preparing a presentation. You are excited, confident, and ready to blow everyone away. But as soon as you finish, your manager says, *"This isn't the right time for this project."* ouch!! That hurts. But instead of sulking, what if you asked, *"Why not?"*. What if you used your manager's feedback to refine your idea and present it again when the timing is right?

My friend, that is the power of 'No'. It helps you learn, makes you resilient, keeps you on your toes, and at times could be irritating, but it tickles your brain with curiosity.

During interviews, one common question you are likely to face is: *"What are your strengths and weaknesses?"*

What's the first thing that comes to mind?

"I am hardworking." "I am trustworthy." "I am a quick learner."

And honestly, that's wonderful, your self-awareness is on point!

But here's a truth we often don't talk about:

Even if you answer everything perfectly, with confidence, clarity, and real-life examples, you might still face rejection.

Why?

Because sometimes, the interviewer is looking for something beyond the basics, qualities that show how you handle pressure, navigate chaos, or stay grounded in adversity.

For example:

"I am quite resilient, especially when the odds are stacked against me."

"I stay rational and logical, even when situations get sticky."

"I thrive on consistency and take pride in delivering stable, dependable results."

See the difference? It's not that your answers were wrong, they just may not have aligned with what the role specifically demanded at that moment.

So, if you are facing rejection, don't let it shake your confidence. It's not a reflection of your worth, talent, or potential. Often, it simply means that your strengths, while absolutely valid may not have matched the current timing, team dynamic, or situational need the employer was looking to fill.

You are not inadequate. You are just being redirected.

The right opportunity will recognize your depth, your values, and the unique energy you bring. Keep showing up with that same honesty, keep refining your narrative, and when the match is right, you will know.

Let's Learn from Birbal's Life Event

Birbal, the wise advisor in Akbar's court, faced rejection all the time. But he never let it stop him. Instead, he used his wit and wisdom to turn 'No' into 'Yes'.

Here is an interesting incident that took place in Akbar's court.

One day in Akbar's court, ministers debated how to manage a new province. While others pushed for strict taxes and fear-based control, Birbal softly suggested,

"Win them with trust. Listen to them, and the revenue will follow." The court laughed. Even Akbar dismissed him.

THE POWER OF 'NO'

"*Not this time, Birbal,*" the emperor said. Birbal bowed, said nothing more, and stepped back. No argument. No ego.

Weeks later, chaos erupted in the province. The harsh approach failed. Farmers revolted, trade slowed, and discontent grew.

Akbar, now worried, called his court again. This time, Birbal simply said,

"*Even the richest soil won't grow if you press too hard. Let it breathe.*"

Akbar nodded. Birbal's way worked. Trust replaced tension. The province flourished.

Here are your key learnings.

1. **Rejection is not personal**

    It's about circumstances, timing, or priorities, not your worth.
    You know what?
    Not Everyone Can Afford a Ferrari!
    In the corporate world, it's not a question of 'if', but 'when'. You will apply for a role and get a 'no'. Share an idea and it won't be picked. Offer help and get ignored. And when that happens, it can feel personal. Like something is wrong with you.
    But here's a thought;
    Have you ever walked past a Ferrari showroom and not bought one?
    Does that mean the Ferrari isn't worth it? Not at all.
    It just means that, at that moment, you were not in a position to take it home.
    Now flip the script.
    You are the Ferrari.
    Rejection doesn't mean you are not valuable. It just means that someone else was not ready for what you bring to the table.
    Maybe the timing was not right. Maybe their needs were different. Maybe their mindset didn't match your horsepower.
    The car doesn't question its worth. And neither should you.

Rejection, especially at work, is more about the fit than the flaw. So the next time you hear a 'No,' don't park your dreams in self-doubt. Instead, remind yourself, *"They just weren't ready for this engine."*

2. 'No' is your best friend

Use 'no' as a chance to learn and improve.

While reading about Einstein, I learnt something interesting about him. The man whose name is now a synonym for genius wasn't exactly welcomed with garlands and standing ovations from day one.

Even Einstein got a 'No', not because he wasn't good enough, but because the world wasn't ready. When he finally rocked the world of physics in 1905 with his theory of relativity, guess what?

The Nobel Prize didn't honour him for that. It was too radical, too hard to prove at the time.

Instead, he was awarded the 1921 Nobel Prize for something more "safe", his work on the photoelectric effect.

But did that stop Einstein ever?

Never!

He used that 'No' as breathing room to think differently.

As motivation to keep pushing.

And as proof that not being accepted right away doesn't mean you are not brilliant.

As you are reading, I am sure there are a lot of instances or events crossing your mind. Do not overthink; instead, channelize your energy to evaluate your worth. Nobody knows you better than you, right? Let's do a Self-Evaluation Activity.

Self-Evaluation Activity

The 'No' Reflection Exercise

Why does this activity matter?

This activity will allow you to shift your mindset from *"I failed"* to *"I learnt."* It teaches you to see rejection as a stepping stone, not a roadblock. By reflecting on your experiences and creating an action plan, you will build **resilience** and **confidence,** two essential traits for thriving in the corporate world.

What do you need to do?

Grab a notebook or open a MS Word document on your computer, and let's get started. (*If you are like me and love to scribble in the book, then add your thoughts in the table.*)

Step	Action	Ask yourself these questions	Respond to your questions
Recall a Recent 'No'	Think about the time you heard 'No' at work. It could be a rejected idea, a missed promotion, or feedback on a project.	• What happened? • How did it make you feel? • What was the reason given for the 'No'?	
Analyse the Situation	Now, let's dig deeper and ask yourself.	• Was the rejection about your idea, or was it about external factors (For example, budget, timing)? • What could you have done differently?	

		• What feedback can you take away from this experience?	
Reframe the 'No'	Here's where the magic happens. Rewrite the story in a positive light.	• How would you feel if you changed the narration? Instead of *"My idea was rejected,"* write, *"My idea wasn't the right fit for this moment, but I learnt how to present it better for next time."* Instead of *"I didn't get the promotion,"* write, *"I now know what skills I need to develop to be ready for the next opportunity."*	
Create an Action Plan	Create a reasonable plan.	Based on your reflection, what should be 2-3 actionable steps you can take to improve or try again? For example: *"I will schedule a meeting with my manager to get detailed feedback on my proposal."* *"I will take a course on project management to strengthen my skills."* *"I will revisit my idea in 3 months when the	

		team has more bandwidth."	
Celebrate Your Growth	The most important part- celebrate your wins, whether small or huge.	Finally, acknowledge your progress. What should you write down about how you handled the situation? For example: *"I stayed professional and didn't let my emotions take over." "I used the feedback to improve my work."*	

Now that you have completed the activity and realized how that one "No", the one that felt so heavy, actually helped you grow, hold on to that insight.

In life, you will probably hear more No's than Yes's.

But each 'No' is not the end; it is just a detour that teaches you, shapes you, and sets you up for something better.

Leverage Birbal's Wisdom in Action

Just like Birbal, you can turn every 'No' into an opportunity, not by magic, but by mastering your mindset.

Rejection will appear in many forms throughout your corporate journey: a resume left unread, an idea overlooked in a meeting, a missed promotion, or feedback that stings. But rejection isn't personal, it's part of the process.

Birbal didn't rise by demanding acceptance; he rose by responding wisely, by observing, learning, adapting, and choosing not to take offense where insight was available.

The real win is not in avoiding the 'No', it's in how you respond when it comes. Every 'No' is a classroom; if you stay present, you will graduate from each one with more clarity, resilience, and self-awareness. So when 'No' knocks next time, don't retreat. Lean in.

> Ask yourself: What is this teaching me? What can I do differently next time? Where can I improve, not just my work, but my attitude and approach?
> Learn to observe without ego, act without fear, and reflect without blame. That's what makes you wise. That's how you grow.
> Rejection is not the opposite of success; it is the soil where future success takes root. Cultivate your rejections, and they will bloom into experiences that no textbook or training can offer.
> As you step into the next chapters of this book and your career, carry this wisdom with you: You are not here to be perfect. You are here to learn, evolve, and lead with presence.
> And if Birbal were standing beside you in your cubicle today, he would probably smile and say, "A 'No' is just a 'Yes' that hasn't understood your potential yet."
> Now, take a breath. Take your lessons. And take the next step forward, smarter, stronger, and unshaken.

Here is a little secret I am sharing with you. Whenever I feel rejected, I read this quote, and it switches my energy.

"IT IS IMPOSSIBLE TO LIVE WITHOUT FAILING AT SOMETHING, UNLESS YOU LIVE SO CAUTIOUSLY THAT YOU MIGHT AS WELL NOT HAVE LIVED AT ALL — IN WHICH CASE, YOU FAIL BY DEFAULT."
— J.K. ROWLING

CHAPTER 2

OFFICE POLITICS
NAVIGATING THE UNSEEN GAME

Remember that school group project where you did most of the work, the research, the slides, and even helped others finish their parts? And then came presentation day, someone else stepped up, spoke confidently, and got all the praise. *Voila!*

You smiled politely. But deep down, did it sting a little?

Ever wondered why credit doesn't always follow effort?

I noticed in my first job something subtle. A few people always seemed to be in the loop, invited to those casual coffee breaks with the manager, laughing at inside jokes, being the first to be considered or chosen for exciting opportunities.

I am sure, just like me, you too must have noticed such events. You were doing good work, too, so what was missing?

Ever paused and thought, *"Is there a game here that no one explained to me?"*

Yes, you were never taught about a game that makes most of us cringe,

OFFICE POLITICS

Yes, it's that quiet, behind-the-scenes dance of power, friendships, and yes, sometimes a little drama too. Whether you are a fan or you would rather avoid it, the truth is, office politics is part of every workplace. But here's something important to remember: it's not all bad.

When you learn to understand and handle it thoughtfully, it can help you build meaningful connections, influence decisions, and open doors for your career. On the flip side, if you ignore it or get tangled up in it the wrong way, it can feel like you are stuck in a messy soap opera, making choices that might hold you back instead of moving you forward.

Picture this:

It's 4:00 p.m., and Seema has survived a marathon of five Zoom meetings and two in-person catch-ups since 10 a.m. Her brain feels fried, and she can almost sense her caffeine reserves running dangerously low. With a tired scratch on her head, she decides to look up from her laptop and take a moment to breathe, a quick coffee break. Honestly, bio-breaks at work might just be the smartest decision anyone can make. Everything else? Totally at the mercy of some stakeholder's whims or that one weird meeting that can flip your whole day upside down.

Seema calls out to her colleague Christina, *"Coffee break?"* And Christina, in her soft, melodic voice, doesn't hesitate. *"I'm slammed today. Only coffee can save me."* Christina hops up, flips her hair, gives a quick eye roll, slumps her shoulder, grabs her strawberry lip balm, and does a lightning-fast touch-up. Because let's be real, no matter how crazy the day, a swipe of lip balm is the easiest trick to looking put together, right? (*My girlies are nodding a big yes!*)

Standing by the pantry, waiting for Babloo *Bhaiya* to pour that steaming cup of magic, the two realize something: they are totally unprepared for tomorrow's big presentation. Cue the synchronized eye rolls and nods. Babloo *Bhaiya's* coffee? No miracle cure here. The caffeine rush won't fix the adrenaline rush that's waiting for them tomorrow. Nope, no way.

Then, just like that, Seema drops her two cents, a spark of an idea that could solve one of the project's trickiest problems. Christina's eyes light up; she's thrilled to hear it. Seema feels a surge of excitement too, this idea might just be her ticket to finally speaking up and building some much-needed credibility in meetings. She's often quiet during discussions, but she knows the feedback to "voice her ideas more" isn't just empty advice. This coffee break conversation? It feels like magic. Tomorrow, she's going to make her mark.

The big day arrives. It's 11:00 a.m., and the team gathers in the meeting room. The energy is thick, everyone looks anxious, confused, and a little lost. Christina, predictably, is busy with one last-minute lip balm touch-up. The boss starts the discussion, and the room falls silent, waiting for ideas to flow.

Seema gathers her courage, ready to speak. But before she can even open her mouth, Christina jumps in with Seema's exact idea. And just like that, Christina steals the spotlight.

The room goes silent, everyone stunned by the brilliance of the suggestion. Seema sits there frozen, a chill running down her spine. Inside, she's screaming, *"Wait! That was my idea! Did she just take my credit?"* It's like Christina baked the cake, then shoved it in her face.

Meanwhile, the idea is a hit, possibly the best solution in the room. Seema imagines herself snapping, maybe scratching Christina's hair or throwing a pie at her face. Her blood is boiling hotter than ever.

As the meeting ends, the team applauds Christina's 'mind-blowing' idea that could save the project, and maybe the world. Seema rushes to the washroom, tears threatening to spill, punching the mirror in frustration. Right now, nothing can cool her anger. But hey, let's not blame Christina. No, let's just blame Babloo *Bhaiya's* coffee. (*This is exactly why I switched from being a coffee person to a full-on tea lover, because my idea got swiped right there, near the coffee vending machine. I still sulk about it sometimes, not going to lie. But trust me, there's a lot to learn from moments like these. So, let's keep going*).

That whole 'Seema–Christina' moment? It could happen to any one of us. You are sitting in a team meeting, and suddenly, a colleague shares an idea that sounds way too familiar, the same one you mentioned to them just last week. But instead of giving you a nod, they act like it's all their own. Ring any bells? Or maybe you have noticed how some folks always seem to land the best projects, even when they are not necessarily the most qualified. Yep, that's office politics showing its face.

Now, before you start daydreaming about some grand revenge (*trust me, don't*), let's shift gears and talk about how to handle this kind of stuff, smartly and strategically. Because here's the truth: you don't have to get sneaky or play dirty to succeed. What you need is a clear, thoughtful approach to navigate the game with your integrity intact.

Let's Learn from Birbal's Life Event

Birbal wasn't new to the tricky world of politics, though in his case, it was the royal court rather than a modern office. Just like in any workplace, there were plenty of jealous courtiers who tried to undermine him or bring him down. But here's the thing: Birbal didn't let their jealousy or petty games get under his skin. Instead of reacting impulsively or stooping to their level, he chose to stay calm and observe what was really going on around him. By paying close attention to the dynamics at play, he could figure out the best way to respond, usually by using his sharp wit and intelligence to quietly outsmart his rivals.

Let me share one story to illustrate this.

One day, a courtier decided to openly challenge Birbal to prove his intelligence. Now, most people might have felt pressured to argue back or defend themselves aggressively, but not Birbal. He took a step back, thought carefully, and came up with a clever riddle.

When he shared it, everyone was amazed, not just by the riddle itself, but by how Birbal handled the challenge with grace and creativity. Instead of wasting time on petty arguments or conflicts, he let his actions and cleverness speak louder than words.

What can we learn from Birbal's approach? It's a reminder that when you face office politics or difficult situations, losing your cool won't help. Staying composed, understanding the situation, and responding thoughtfully sometimes with a bit of humour or cleverness can help you maintain your integrity and actually come out ahead. (*while I am writing this, I am still learning this art*).

In other words, it's about playing smart, not playing dirty.

Here are your key learnings.

1. **Office politics is inevitable**
   It's part of human nature, especially in a competitive environment. Think of office politics like the currents in the ocean. You may not always see them on the surface, but they are always there, quietly influencing the direction of everything around. Whether you are swimming with the flow or trying to go your own way, you can't pretend the current doesn't exist, it's just part of the environment.
   Similarly, in any workplace, especially a competitive one, office politics is a natural part of the human experience. Where there are people, there are opinions, ambitions, alliances, and sometimes, silent power plays.
   The key isn't to avoid it altogether (*because you can't*), but to learn how to navigate it without losing yourself. Just like a skilled swimmer reads the water before diving in, a mindful professional observes the dynamics, understands the undercurrents, and moves wisely.

2. **Stay neutral**
   Avoid taking sides or getting involved in gossip.
   Imagine you are in the middle of a bonfire night, cozy, warm, and beautiful from a distance. But the moment you get too close to the flames, you risk getting burned. That's what gossip and office cliques can feel like. They might seem harmless at first, just casual chats or shared frustrations but if you are not careful, you can find yourself tangled in someone else's fire.
   That's why staying neutral is such a powerful and wise choice. It doesn't mean being passive or disconnected. It means being

mindful of your energy and your words. It means choosing not to take sides in conflicts that don't involve you directly, and resisting the tempting pull of workplace gossip, no matter how juicy it sounds.

When you choose neutrality, you protect your credibility. People start seeing you as someone trustworthy, level-headed, and emotionally mature, someone they can rely on for clarity, not chaos. In the long run, that kind of quiet strength carries more influence than any dramatic alliance ever could.

3. **Focus on relationships**

   Build genuine connections based on trust and respect.

   Think of relationships at work like tending to a little office garden. You can't just show up during harvest season expecting fruits if you haven't taken time to plant, water, and nurture the seeds. In the world of office politics, genuine relationships are your strongest roots. When you build connections based on trust, mutual respect, and not just convenience, you create a support system that can weather any storm, even the passive-aggressive email kind.

   It's easy to network for favours, but it's far more powerful to connect for real. Remember, people may forget what you said in a meeting, but they won't forget how you made them feel during a tough day. So, instead of plotting power moves, focus on people. Because in the long run, authentic relationships outlast temporary alliances, and they make the journey a whole lot more enjoyable too.

4. **Let your work speak for itself**

   Your performance is your best defence against office politics.

   Let's take a moment here, have you ever met someone who didn't say much in meetings or are quite logical in what they say or are very disciplined with work ethics but consistently delivered amazing work? The kind of person who quietly earns respect without chasing the spotlight? That's the power of letting your work speak for itself.

In the noise of office politics, where some voices are louder than others, your performance is your quiet, steady anchor. You don't always need to fight for attention or get involved in every conversation. When your work is consistent, thoughtful, and reliable, it naturally builds credibility, and credibility is the one thing politics can't shake.

So here's a gentle nudge: focus on showing up fully for your responsibilities. Be the one who follows through, who adds value, who solves problems. That's your silent yet powerful response to any behind-the-scenes drama. Because while words can be twisted, results rarely are.

And ask yourself: *"What story is my work telling today?"*

As you are progressing with each chapter, I am sure a few faces, moments, and maybe even some "ouch" memories are popping into your head. That's completely okay, it means you are reflecting, and that's a powerful first step.

After all, who knows your journey, challenges, and wins better than you?

Let's press pause and do a little self-check, an honest, gentle look at where you stand. Ready? Let's dive into a Self-Evaluation Activity.

Self-Evaluation Activity

The Office Politics Map

This activity will help you understand the power dynamics in your workplace and navigate them effectively.

Why does this activity matter?

This activity helps you become more aware of the invisible forces at play in your workplace. By understanding the power dynamics and motivations of key players, you can navigate office politics with confidence and integrity. Remember, the goal isn't to manipulate

OFFICE POLITICS

others, it's to build positive relationships and create a supportive environment for yourself.

What do you need to do?

Feel free to keep jotting down your thoughts in your notebook, or if you're comfortable, scribble right here in the book!

Step	What to do?	Respond to your questions.
Identify Key Players	Think about your workplace and list the key influencers. These could be: • Formal Leaders: Managers, Team Leads, or Executives. • Informal Leaders: Colleagues who may not have a title but have influence (For example: the person everyone goes to for advice). • Alliances: Groups or cliques that often work together.	
Map Relationships	Draw lines to show how these players are connected. For example: • Who has a strong relationship with the boss? • Who often collaborates with whom? • Are there any visible rivalries or conflicts?	
Analyse Motivations	For each key player, ask yourself: • What are their goals?	

	• What do they value (For example: recognition, power, teamwork)? • How do they prefer to communicate (For example: formal emails or casual chats)?	
Plan Your Approach	Based on your map, think about how you can build positive relationships with key players. For example: • If your manager values data-driven decisions, make sure to back up your ideas with facts. • If a colleague is influential but loves recognition, give them credit for their contributions. • If there's a rivalry between two teams, stay neutral and focus on your work.	
Reflect and Adjust	After a week, revisit your map and reflect: • Did your approach work? • Are there any new dynamics you need to consider? • What can you do differently next time?	

Now that you have completed this activity, you might have noticed something important: sometimes, our own ego can be the biggest obstacle when navigating office politics. Recognizing this is a huge step forward because it opens the door for growth, through genuine connections and thoughtful progress.

Keep in mind, building relationships doesn't mean compromising your integrity. It's not about chasing favours or flattering others. It's about showing up authentically and doing the right things consistently. When you focus on that, connections naturally follow, and so does meaningful progress.

Leverage Birbal's Wisdom in Action

As we wrap up this chapter on office politics, let's pause and reflect on the timeless wisdom of Birbal- the master of navigating tricky court politics with grace, wit, and a cool head. Birbal's success wasn't because he played dirty or outshouted everyone else. It was because he stayed calm, stayed observant, and played smart. And here's the good news: you can do the same.

Think of office politics not as a battlefield, but as a strategic game, like chess or a puzzle. You don't win by rushing in blindly or reacting to every move your opponents make. You win by watching the whole board, understanding the players, and thinking a few moves ahead. Birbal never let the noise and drama distract him; he stayed focused on his values and used his intelligence to solve problems creatively.

Ask yourself: *Are you rushing to react, or are you pausing to understand? Are you getting caught in petty fights, or are you choosing your battles wisely? Are you trying to impress by flattery or chasing favours, or are you building genuine relationships based on trust and respect?*

The truth is, office politics is inevitable; it's part of human nature whenever people work closely together with ambitions and emotions at play. But that doesn't mean you have to lose yourself or compromise your integrity to succeed. You don't have to play dirty to win; you just need to play smart.

Building your career is more like planting a tree than running a race. It takes patience, care, and steady effort. When you choose to act with wisdom, observe with curiosity, and connect with authenticity, you create a foundation that's strong enough to withstand any storm, and that kind of strength lasts.

> So, as you step back into your workplace, bring a little of Birbal's spirit with you. Stay calm in the chaos, be strategic in your moves, and most importantly, stay true to who you are. When you do, you won't just survive office politics, you will thrive in it.
>
> And remember: playing smart doesn't mean playing alone. Reach out, build bridges, and learn from every interaction. Because sometimes, the best victories come from collaboration, not competition.
>
> Now, take a deep breath, gather your thoughts, and get ready to step into your next meeting, Birbal style.

Time to share a secret again and I will keep sharing it at the end of every chapter. Whenever I feel side-lined or overlooked in office politics, I turn to this quote, it never fails to shift my mindset and boost my energy.

It's a reminder to not take office politics too seriously, keep your sense of humour, and focus on what really matters: your own integrity and growth.

"POLITICS IS THE ART OF LOOKING FOR TROUBLE, FINDING IT EVERYWHERE, DIAGNOSING IT INCORRECTLY, AND APPLYING THE WRONG REMEDIES."
— GROUCHO MARX

CHAPTER 3
PERCEPTION BUILDING
YOUR IMAGE MATTERS

You walk into the office wearing your usual comfortable outfit, feeling confident and ready for the day. Later, during a casual conversation, a colleague mentions, *"You look different today, more professional."* Suddenly, you realize that the way you present yourself can change how others see your abilities and potential.

- *How much do you think your appearance and demeanour influence the way people perceive your competence?*
- *Could small changes in how you 'show up' impact your career growth, even if your skills remain the same?*
- *What image do you want to create at work, and how are you currently shaping it?*
- *How often do you think image or first impressions tip the scales in professional settings?*
- *What aspects of your behaviour or style could you refine to better reflect your true capabilities?*
- *How can you balance being authentic with the need to manage how others perceive you?*

Let's talk about something that might feel a little uncomfortable but is super important,

HOW OTHERS SEE YOU - PERCEPTION

Riya was sharp, efficient, and quietly consistent. She delivered on deadlines, double-checked her data, and made sure her teammates never had to cover for her. Her desk was a little clutter, okay, maybe more than a little, and she preferred wearing comfortable kurtis and floaters to the crisp blazers and heels that many of her peers wore.

PERCEPTION BUILDING

She believed in one thing: *"Good work will speak for itself."*

But then came the moment that shook that belief a little.

It was the monthly business review meeting. Riya had worked tirelessly on a data dashboard that simplified a previously messy process. She had been up till 2 a.m. perfecting the formula logic and colour codes. She knew her stuff inside out.

Yet, when the meeting began, her manager barely looked in her direction. Instead, all eyes were on Arjun, the ever-so-charming team member who, let's be honest, knew some of the work but all of the right things to say. He had volunteered to "present on behalf of the team." Riya hadn't objected. She thought, as long as the project gets noticed, it's fine.

But something stung.

As Arjun went on to explain the dashboard, taking a few creative liberties and skipping the part where Riya single-handedly designed the entire thing, the room responded with approving nods and praise. The boss even said, *"Great initiative, Arjun."*

Riya sat there, lips pursed, heart quietly sinking.

Later That Day…

Over coffee, Riya spoke to her friend Shalini from HR.

"You know," she said, *"it's funny. You can be the one doing the heavy lifting, but unless you market yourself, it's like you are invisible."*

Shalini smiled. *"That's not funny, it's reality. In the corporate world, perception often outweighs reality. It's not just about what you do, it's about how others perceive what you do."*

She continued, *"I have seen average performers get fast-tracked simply because they dress sharp, speak up in meetings, and seem confident, even when they are unsure. Meanwhile, some brilliant minds, like you, sit in the back thinking their work will speak."*

PERCEPTION BUILDING

Riya looked away. *"But I don't want to pretend or act fake."*

"No one's asking you to," Shalini said gently. *"There's a difference between being authentic and being careless about how you present yourself. Your image is your professional currency. It's what people remember when you are not in the room."*

Fast Forward Two Weeks....

Riya made some small changes. She started speaking up in meetings, just once or twice, but enough to be noticed. She wore slightly more formal clothes, still herself, just a polished version. She began taking the lead on presenting her own work. Not bragging, just owning.

It wasn't overnight, but people started noticing. Her manager began calling on her directly in meetings. Colleagues came to her for insights. And Arjun? Still charming, still loud, but no longer the only one who got the spotlight.

You see, in the corporate world, perception often outweighs reality. It's not just about what you do, it's about how others perceive what you do. And here's the kicker: You can be the most talented person in the room, but if people don't see you that way, it won't matter.

Think about it.

Have you ever noticed how some colleagues always seem to get the spotlight, even if their work isn't necessarily better than yours? Or, how someone who dresses well and speaks confidently is often perceived as more capable, even if their skills are average? That's the power of perception.

Now, I am not saying you should become someone you are not. Authenticity is key. But there's a difference between being authentic and being careless about how you present yourself.

Your professional image is like your personal brand; it's what people think of when they hear your name. And just like any brand, it needs to be managed.

PERCEPTION BUILDING

Let's Learn from Birbal's Life Event

One fine morning in Emperor Akbar's court, a strange complaint arrived.

A wealthy merchant, puffed up with frustration, stood before the emperor and said, *"Your Majesty, I have been robbed. Someone stole my prized donkey!"*

The court erupted in mild amusement. A donkey?

Akbar raised an eyebrow. *"Why is this donkey so important to you?"*

The merchant explained, *"He was not just any donkey. He was trained, obedient, and could even follow commands like a horse! I painted him with red and gold stripes to make him easy to recognize."*

Akbar glanced around the court. *"Who among you will solve this riddle of the missing, painted donkey?"*

Some courtiers chuckled and looked away. It didn't seem like a matter worth their intellect.

But Birbal, as always, stepped forward.

"Give me three days, Your Majesty," he said calmly. *"I will find the donkey."*

Day One

Birbal didn't rush. Instead, he strolled through the marketplace, visited tea stalls, and spoke with local children, weavers, and potters. No questions about a donkey, just casual chats. Observing. Listening. Letting people be themselves around him.

Word spread: Birbal is investigating something. People became alert without knowing why.

Day Two

He quietly asked the town criers to shout:

PERCEPTION BUILDING

"Anyone who hides a painted donkey shall be cursed for seven generations!"

People chuckled. Still, curiosity brewed.

Day Three – At the Court

Birbal entered the court with a smile and a scroll in hand.

"Your Majesty, the donkey is with the cobbler near the southern gate. He tried to wash off the paint and disguise it as a stray."

Akbar was stunned. *"How did you find out without asking anyone directly?"*

Birbal bowed slightly. *"Perception, Your Majesty. When people see someone calmly paying attention, they begin to behave differently. I didn't chase the answer. I made space for it to come to me. I let my presence do half the work."*

What did Birbal do here?

Birbal didn't solve the case with drama. He didn't storm into homes or make noise. He simply carried the image of a man who could not be fooled, and that made people nervous enough to reveal the truth themselves.

His calm, consistent demeanour created an aura of reliability and intelligence, a perception that gave him power without pressure.

In the workplace, you don't need to shout to be seen. You don't need to constantly prove your worth. But you do need to carry yourself with quiet confidence. Show up consistently. Be calm under pressure. Let people associate your name with trust, wit, and wisdom.

Here are your key learnings.

1. **Perception is reality**
   How others see you can impact your career more than your actual performance.

PERCEPTION BUILDING

Think of Yourself as a Book on a Shelf

Imagine you are a book placed among many others on a shelf in a bookstore. You know your pages are filled with depth, stories of hard work, ideas, creativity, and resilience.

But here's the truth: most people won't read your content right away. They will glance at your cover, maybe read the blurb, and only then decide if they want to pick you up.

Now, is it fair to judge a book by its cover? Probably not. *But do people do it?* All the time.

That's what perception is in the workplace. It's your cover, your title, your blurb. It's how you carry yourself, how you speak in meetings, how you respond to pressure, and even how you show up when no one's watching.

It doesn't mean the inside, the real you, doesn't matter. It does. But to get people to open the book and truly appreciate the content, they need a reason to pick it up first.

So, ask yourself:

- *What does my "cover" say about me at work?*
- *Am I being intentional about how I show up, or leaving it to chance?*
- *What would I want people to say about me when I am not in the room?*

Perception doesn't mean faking it. It means aligning your inner values with how you outwardly present yourself, so people see the true potential you bring to the table.

2. Be intentional

Your appearance, communication, and behaviour all contribute to your professional image.

You Are Your Own Walking Billboard

Every day when you step into work, whether in person or virtually, you are putting up a sign that tells the world something about who you are. The way you dress, the words you choose, and the way you respond to emails or join conversations in meetings. These are all messages flashing across your billboard.

Now here's the question:

Are you designing that message thoughtfully, or are you letting random impressions take over the space?

Imagine if a brand you love, say your favourite coffee shop or clothing label, randomly changed its colours, logo, or tone of voice every other day. You would probably start to feel confused or unsure about what they stood for, right? The same goes for you in the workplace. Consistency, clarity, and intention matter.

Being intentional doesn't mean being rigid or fake. It means showing up in a way that reflects the best version of who you already are, on purpose. If you want to be seen as dependable, collaborative, or innovative, think about how your daily actions and presence can reinforce that.

Ask yourself:

- *Does my tone reflect the confidence I feel inside?*
- *Is my attire aligning with how I want to be perceived?*
- *Am I communicating in a way that supports the image I want to build?*

You don't have to be perfect, you just have to be intentional. And little by little, those intentional choices shape the reputation people come to associate with your name.

3. **Consistency is key**

As said, consistency is the game changer. Your actions should align with the image you want to project.

You are a Daily Newspaper - What's Your Headline?

Imagine you are the editor of a daily newspaper. Every morning, your "headline" shows up for your co-workers, managers, and team members to read. It might not be written in ink, but it's loud and clear through your actions, words, and presence.

Now ask yourself:

- *What headline are you consistently printing?*
- *Is it "Reliable. Shows up. Delivers on time"?*

PERCEPTION BUILDING

- *Or is it "Great one day, missing the next"?*

Here's the thing: one great edition won't define you. Just like a newspaper builds its reputation over time, so do you. If you want to be seen as dependable, innovative, or collaborative, you have to make sure your daily editions reflect that.

Think of someone you admire at work. Chances are, it's not just because they did something impressive once; it's because they show up in that same powerful, positive way again and again. That's the power of consistency. It builds trust, credibility, and yes, even influence.

A little reflection for you:

- *"Are your everyday actions echoing the image you want to build"?*
- *"Would your 'headline" match your intention"?*

Remember, consistency isn't about being robotic or perfect. It's about showing up with intention and steadiness so people know exactly what to expect when they hear your name.

As we journey through this chapter on perception, you have probably begun to notice some patterns, maybe a colleague who always gets noticed, or a moment where your great work somehow went unnoticed. Maybe you have caught yourself thinking, *"Why does no one see the effort I put in?"*

Don't worry, you are not alone. These thoughts are part of the process. Recognizing them means you are starting to see things not just as they are, but how they appear to others. That shift in perspective? It's gold.

This next part is all about you - your story, your image, your truth.

So, let's pause. Take a breath. And gently explore how you are showing up and how you'd like to be seen. No pressure, just honest reflection.

Ready? Let's begin your Self-Evaluation Activity.

PERCEPTION BUILDING

Self-Evaluation Activity

THE PERCEPTION AUDIT

Why does this activity matter?

This activity helps you take control of your professional image. By being intentional about how you present yourself, you can build a reputation that aligns with your goals and values.

Remember, your image is not just about looking good, it's about creating a lasting impression that opens doors for your career.

What do you need to do?

Fill in your response in the table or continue writing in your notepad.

Step	What to do?	Respond to your questions.
Define Your Desired Image	Think about how you want to be perceived at work. For example: • *Do you want to be seen as a leader, a problem-solver, or a team player?* • *What qualities do you want people to associate with you (For example - reliable, innovative, approachable)?* Write down 3-5 words that describe your desired professional image.	
Assess Your Current Image	Now, let's see how others perceive you. Ask yourself: • *How do I currently present myself at work?*	

	• *What feedback have I received from colleagues or managers?* • *Are there any gaps between how I want to be seen and how I am seen?* If you are not sure, consider asking a trusted colleague or mentor for honest feedback.	
Identify Areas for Improvement	Based on your assessment, identify specific areas where you can improve. For example: • Appearance: *Do you dress appropriately for your role and organization?* • Communication: *Do you speak clearly and confidently in meetings and emails?* • Behaviour: *Do your actions align with your desired image* (For example - being punctual, reliable, and professional)?	
Create an Action Plan	Write down 2-3 actionable steps to improve your professional image. For example: *"I will dress more professionally by wearing business attire to important meetings."* *"I will align my actions with my desired image by being more punctual and reliable."*	
Monitor Your Progress	After a month, revisit your action plan and reflect:	

	• *Have you noticed any changes in how others perceive you?* • *Are there any new areas for improvement?* • *What can you do to continue building your professional image?*	

You know, I've often heard people at work say, *"Oh, I don't build perceptions about anyone."* And every time, I smile a little, because whether we realize it or not, we all do it.

We notice how someone dresses, how they speak, how they eat their lunch, how they handle pressure or deadlines. Every little action silently contributes to how we see others, and how they see us.

That's why being intentional about how you show up matters. It's not about being fake; it's about being aware. So yes, perception-building isn't just some corporate buzzword. It's your personal brand in motion. And you have got the power to shape it; wisely and authentically.

Leverage Birbal's Wisdom in Action

As we wrap up this chapter on perception building, let's take a moment to reflect, not just on what you have read, but on how it lands in your everyday life.

In the corporate world, much like in Akbar's court, it's not just about what you do, it's also about how the world sees you doing it. And nobody knew how to manage that better than Birbal.

Birbal didn't walk around boasting about his intelligence or demanding respect. He earned it. Through his calm presence, thoughtful words, and unwavering consistency, he built a reputation that spoke louder than any self-promotion ever could. That's exactly the kind of professional image that stands the test of time - subtle, authentic, yet powerfully effective.

Now think about your image. You don't have to be the loudest voice in the room to be remembered. You don't have to be flashy to be respected. What you do need is intentionality. When you dress the part, speak with clarity, act with integrity, and stay consistent in how you show up, people notice. You slowly start to build a brand of trust, reliability, and credibility.

Remember, perception isn't about pretending to be someone else. It's about presenting your best self, consistently. Your skills matter, but so does the package they come in. And this package, your personal brand, is something you curate every single day.

So, as you move forward in your career, channel your inner Birbal. Be strategic, not manipulative. Be visible, not loud. And most importantly, be authentic. Because your image is your brand, and it's worth investing in.

Let your work shine, let your actions speak, and let your presence reflect the values you stand for. That's how you create a perception that not only opens doors but earns respect when you walk through them.

When I was around 12, I came across a quote that stuck with me for life. It may sound simple, but I have lived by those words, and let me tell you, it really does make a difference.

"RIGHT ATTITUDE, WITH RIGHT APTITUDE, WILL TAKE YOU TO THE RIGHT ALTITUDE."

CHAPTER 4
RECOGNITION VS. DILIGENCE
THE UNSUNG HEROES PATH

Let's be honest, life in the corporate world comes with its own set of rules, and not all of them are written down. One of them is,

<u>YOUR HARD WORK WON'T ALWAYS BE RECOGNIZED</u>

Let's pause for a reality check. You have been showing up, early mornings, late nights, pouring your energy into every task, staying one step ahead, going the extra mile. Not because someone asked, but because that's who you are, driven, dedicated, and quietly committed to excellence.

But despite your effort, there's silence.

No *"Well done."*

No *"Thank you."*

Not even a passing nod in the hallway.

Sound familiar?

It's disheartening, right? You start asking yourself, *"What's the point of giving my best if no one seems to care?"* That creeping sense of invisibility can sting deeper than any feedback ever could. And this isn't just about wanting a pat on the back, it's about being seen, being valued, and feeling like your contribution counts.

Here's where the wisdom comes in.

In the corporate world, recognition doesn't always walk hand-in-hand with effort. It should, but often, it doesn't. That doesn't mean your work is any less meaningful. It means you may need to rethink how you are making your impact visible. Not louder, just clearer.

This chapter isn't about chasing applause or demanding attention. It's about understanding how recognition works, where it often gets misdirected, and how you can stay rooted in your purpose while finding your own path to being seen and appreciated. Because yes, you deserve to be recognized. Not just for what you do, but for who you are when no one's watching.

Sometimes, the lack of recognition isn't because you are not doing enough, it could be that your manager is juggling a thousand things and just doesn't see the full picture. Or maybe, someone else is quicker to speak up and take credit. And yes, there are days when it feels downright unfair. We have all been there, haven't we?

But take a deep breath and hold this close: your effort, your diligence - it does matter, even when it feels invisible.

Take a second and really think about it. The people who rise steadily in their careers aren't always the loudest in the room. They are the ones who keep showing up, doing the right thing, and staying true to their craft, even when no one's clapping. They are the quiet warriors, the consistent performers, the ones who may not always be seen, but are always making a difference.

Let's explore how to navigate this quiet gap between effort and acknowledgment, with the poise of Birbal and the clarity of someone who knows their worth.

Let's Learn from Birbal's Life Event

It was spring in the Mughal Empire, and Emperor Akbar had declared that the royal gardens should be made ready for a grand festival. Ministers, nobles, and even visiting kings would walk through the gardens. Every tree, shrub, and flowerbed needed to be in perfect bloom.

The task of supervising the garden was given to a group of royal courtiers. They were excited, after all, this was a chance to impress the emperor and maybe earn a few jewels or a new title. Each day, they came dressed in fine robes, walked around with scrolls, gave orders to the gardeners, and spoke loudly about how hard they were working.

Birbal observed quietly from a distance. He noticed one old gardener named Gopal who didn't speak much. He came before sunrise, watered the plants, trimmed with care, pulled out weeds by hand, and left quietly long after sunset.

No one praised him. No one noticed. In fact, some courtiers often stepped right past him, barely acknowledging his presence.

Finally, the day of the festival arrived. Akbar strolled through the garden with his guests, admiring the vibrant colours and heavenly scents. The guests were full of praise. Akbar beamed with pride.

He called forward the courtiers who had been assigned the task. "*You have done well,*" he said. "*Ask for a reward.*"

Each man stepped forward, claiming credit in elegant words, some spoke of their management, others of their design choices, and a few even recited poetries about flowers.

Just then, Birbal stepped forward and whispered something in Akbar's ear.

The emperor smiled, and without saying a word, called for the guards.

Moments later, the old gardener Gopal was brought in, confused and still wearing his muddy kurta.

Akbar looked at the courtiers. "*You all spoke of your leadership and efforts, but I asked my guards to watch who truly worked day and night in this garden. This man did not ask for recognition. He did not claim credit. Yet the results of his work speak louder than any poetry.*"

Turning to Gopal, Akbar said, *"You are the true architect of this beauty. And though you never asked, today, I give you the honour due."*

Gopal bowed humbly, tears in his eyes, not because of the gift of gold that followed, but because his quiet work had been seen at last.

So what's the lesson for you, dear reader?

Like Gopal, there will be times in your journey when your effort goes unnoticed. You may feel invisible while others speak louder, shine brighter, or claim credit for what you helped build. You might wonder, *"Why bother if no one sees me?"*

But remember this - diligence is never wasted.

Recognition may not come instantly, but the respect you build through consistent, quality work becomes your silent, unshakable strength. People may not clap every day, but they notice, and when it matters most, your integrity will speak for you.

Just like Birbal knew the value of Gopal's silence, someone wise will notice yours too.

So, keep going. Keep giving. And let your work bloom, even when no one's watching.

Here are your key learnings.

1. **Recognition isn't guaranteed**
    Your hard work may not always be noticed, but that doesn't mean it's not valuable.
    Think of a tree. What do you see? The tall trunk, the spreading branches, the lush green leaves. That's the visible part, the part that gets admired, photographed, and appreciated.
    But what truly holds that tree steady? The roots.
    Deep underground, out of sight, the roots work silently. They anchor the tree, absorb nutrients, and help it grow tall and strong. No one claps for the roots. No one even sees them.
    But without them, the tree wouldn't survive a single storm.

Your hard work, your late nights, your quiet contributions, your diligence, are just like those roots.

You may not always get recognition, but you are building something far more powerful: stability, growth, and long-term success.

So stay rooted. Your strength will eventually show in the way you rise.

2. **Focus on the long game**

    Consistency and diligence will pay off, even if it takes time.

    Picture a potter at work.

    He sits patiently, shaping a lump of clay on a spinning wheel. At first glance, it just looks messy, hands muddy, no sign of beauty. But the potter knows something we often forget: real transformation takes time.

    He doesn't rush. He adds water gently, adjusts the pressure, and keeps the wheel turning. Bit by bit, the shape forms. Not all at once but through consistent effort, guided hands, and patience. Finally, when the pot is complete, it's strong, balanced, and beautiful. Ready to be admired and used for years to come.

    That's what your career journey is like.

    You might not see instant results. You might feel like the spotlight is always on someone else. But if you stay consistent, keep showing up with integrity, and focus on your craft, your moment will come. And when it does, you will not only be seen, you will be remembered.

    So play the long game. Greatness is rarely rushed - it's shaped.

3. **Document your achievements**

    Keep a record of your contributions to ensure you get credit when it matters.

    Think of yourself as an architect designing a remarkable building. Day by day, you create blueprints, supervise construction, solve on-the-spot challenges, and ensure the structure is safe and stunning. But unlike the ribbon-cutting ceremony, where speeches are made and photos are taken, most of your hard work happens quietly, behind the scenes.

Now imagine, months later, when the building is complete, someone asks, *"Who made this possible?"*

If you didn't document your plans, sign your designs, or leave a trail of your involvement, your name could be left out of the credits. Not out of malice, but simply because there's no record.

That's why successful professionals act like architects: they keep blueprints of their contributions. Not to boast, but to make sure their work stands tall when it matters, during performance reviews, promotions, or job transitions.

In your career, many of your best efforts will go unnoticed unless you take the initiative to track them. A well-kept record is not vanity, it's visibility. It's a reminder that your journey has structure, strength, and story.

As you reflect on these important lessons, how recognition isn't always guaranteed, why playing the long game matters, and the power of keeping track of your wins - take a moment to pause. These aren't just abstract ideas; they are practical steps you can apply in your own journey.

Remember, your hard work has value, even when it feels unseen. Staying consistent results into the foundation for your success, and having a clear record of your achievements ensures your efforts don't get lost in the noise.

Now, let's turn the spotlight inward. It's time for a little self-check, an honest, gentle look at where you stand and how you can make your hard work shine brighter.

Ready to dive in? Let's start this Self-Evaluation Activity together.

RECOGNITION VS. DILIGENCE

Self-Evaluation Activity

THE UNSUNG HEROES JOURNAL

Why does this activity matter?

This exercise helps you stay motivated and focused, even when your hard work goes unnoticed.

By documenting your achievements, you will have a clear record of your contributions, which can be invaluable during performance reviews or when advocating for yourself. Plus, celebrating your wins, big or small, will keep you motivated and remind you of your value.

What do you need to do?

You already know the drill if you have come this far. Continue to jot down your response.

Step	What to do?	Respond to your questions.
Reflect on Your Work	Think about the past month and write down: • What projects or tasks did you work on? • What challenges did you overcome? • What impact did your work have (For example - *improved processes, helped a colleague, met a deadline*)?	
Acknowledge Your Efforts	For each task or project, write down: • What you're proud of (For example - "*I stayed late to finish*	

	the report and ensured it was error-free"). • What you learned (For example - "*I improved my time management skills*").
Document Your Achievements	Create a "Winner file" to keep track of your accomplishments. Include: • Specific examples of your work (For example - "*Led a team to complete Project X ahead of schedule*"). • Received Positive feedback from colleagues or clients (For example - "*Client praised my presentation skills*"). • On track with metrics or results (For example - "*Increased sales by 10% through my marketing strategy*").
Set Goals for the Future	Based on your reflection, write down 2-3 goals for the next month. For example: • "*I will take on a leadership role in the upcoming project.*" • "*I will improve my public speaking skills by presenting in team meetings.*" • "*I will document my contributions weekly to ensure I'm prepared for my next performance review.*"

Celebrate Your Wins	At the end of each week, take a moment to celebrate your achievements, no matter how small. For example: • *"I finished the report ahead of schedule, superb!"* • *"I received positive feedback from my manager, time to treat myself!"*

As you wrap up this self-evaluation, take a moment to reflect on a timeless teaching that has guided countless seekers and leaders alike, a verse from the Shrimad Bhagavad Gita.

The Sanskrit verse;

कर्मण्येवाधिकारस्ते मा फलेषु कदाचन |

मा कर्मफलहेतुर्भूर्मा ते सङ्गोऽस्त्वकर्मणि ||

Translation of this verse (taken from Shrimad Bhagavad Gita)

You have the right to perform your duties, but you are not entitled to the fruits of your actions. Hence, focus on your duties, detach yourself from the results, and serve with selfless action.

This teaching reminds us that our true power lies not in chasing recognition or rewards, but in dedicating ourselves fully to the work at hand, without being attached to what comes next. It's a call to become a *Karmyogi*, someone who performs their duty with unwavering focus, integrity, and selflessness.

Of course, this is easier said than done. Our minds naturally want appreciation, praise, and validation. But through conscious practice, we can retrain ourselves to embrace the process over the outcome. This shift frees us from anxiety and frustration and opens the door to greater creativity, resilience, and satisfaction in our work.

RECOGNITION VS. DILIGENCE

By living this wisdom, you position yourself not only for success but for a deeper sense of purpose and peace amid the ups and downs of the corporate world. So as you move forward, remember: it's the quality of your effort, not the applause it earns, that defines your journey.

Keep this verse close to your heart as you continue to build your path, and let it inspire you to work diligently, stay humble, and trust that the results will follow in their own time.

Leverage Birbal's Wisdom in Action

If there's one thing history teaches us through Birbal's stories, it's this: consistency and integrity are your secret weapons, no magic potion needed. Birbal wasn't always in the spotlight, but his steady wisdom and honest approach earned him a place in the emperor's inner circle, proving that slow and steady often wins the race.

Think of your career the same way. Sure, sometimes it feels like you are working hard in the shadows, while others bask in the limelight. But here's a little secret: real influence isn't about flash or fanfare. It's about showing up day after day, doing your best, and holding on to your values even when no one's clapping.

The "unsung hero" might sound like a title reserved for background characters, but in reality, it's the crown worn by those who build rock-solid credibility. Your efforts may go unnoticed for now, but they are quietly laying the foundation for future success - like seeds growing strong roots beneath the surface.

So, channel your inner Birbal. Stay patient, stay authentic, and keep doing great work. The applause might not be immediate, but trust me, your diligence will make you unforgettable in the long run. Because in the game of corporate chess, it's not just about making moves, it's about making the right moves consistently.

And hey, if Birbal could outwit the entire court with a calm smile and sharp wit, you can definitely outlast a few quiet days at work, right? Keep at it, the best is yet to come.

I recall a quote at this moment, whenever I speak about recognition versus diligence, it helps me stay grounded and patient.

> "SUCCESS IS NOT BUILT ON SUCCESS. IT'S BUILT ON FAILURE, FRUSTRATION, AND SOMETIMES EVEN CATASTROPHE."
> — SUMNER REDSTONE

CHAPTER 5

WORK ETHICS AND INTEGRITY
THE CORNERSTONES OF SUCCESS

Alright, let's get straight to the heart of the matter:

WORK ETHICS AND INTEGRITY

Fancy words, right? But believe me, these two aren't just some corporate jargon or buzzwords tossed around in boardrooms. They are the real deal, the bedrock on which every solid career is built. Think of them as the secret sauce that turns your hard work into lasting success.

But here's the catch: playing by the rules and doing the "right thing" isn't always the easiest path. Sometimes it feels like the hardest. You are probably wondering why anyone would want to make life difficult for themselves when there's a shortcut just waiting to be taken. Well, the answer is simple, because shortcuts in ethics rarely lead to long-term wins. And if you think otherwise, just ask the countless stories of careers that crumbled overnight.

Picture this:

It's Friday afternoon, and your manager slides a report across your desk, asking you to *"just tweak a few numbers"* so the quarter looks better. Or maybe a co-worker nudges you, saying, *"Hey, let's both take credit for that project you led. Boss loves teamwork, right?"* Suddenly, your integrity is on the line, and your next move feels like a high-stakes game of corporate Jenga. One wrong move, and everything could come crashing down.

Now, let me ask you - *what would you do?*

It's tempting, isn't it? To take the easy way out, to avoid the awkward conversation, to keep your head down and just go with the flow. But here's the thing: those little compromises?

They don't stay little for long. One fudge here, one shortcut there, before you know it, you are stuck in a maze of half-truths, unearned credit, and sleepless nights.

The truth is, your reputation in the workplace is like a finely tuned instrument. One scratch, one misplaced note, and it's hard to regain that perfect pitch. But when you consistently play with honesty, reliability, and fairness, your reputation becomes a powerful melody that others want to hear and trust. It's what sets you apart when the spotlight is on, and what holds you steady when the going gets tough.

Here's the good news: integrity isn't about being perfect. It's about being intentional. It's about choosing, moment by moment, to stand for what's right, even when no one's watching. Because, at the end of the day, the most valuable currency in the corporate world isn't your latest project or your LinkedIn endorsements. It's trust. And trust? That takes time, courage, and consistent action to build.

So, as you move forward, remember this: Work ethic and integrity may not always get you the loudest applause or the fastest promotions. But they will get you something far more important, a career you can be proud of, a network that respects you, and a self-respect that no one can take away.

Ready to dive deeper? Let's explore how you can keep these cornerstones solid, no matter what the corporate jungle throws your way – the Birbal way.

Let's Learn from Birbal's Life Event

In the grand court of Emperor Akbar, where brilliance and politics intertwined like the intricate patterns on a royal tapestry, Birbal stood out not just for his wit but for his unwavering integrity. Known far and wide as the wise advisor who could solve any riddle, Birbal had a reputation for never compromising on what he believed was right, even if it meant standing alone against the mighty emperor himself.

One day, the emperor summoned Birbal for a task that tested more than just his cleverness. Akbar had made a decision, one that many in the court felt was unjust. It was about a local merchant accused of cheating in a trade deal. The evidence was thin, but Akbar, under pressure from some powerful courtiers, had decided to punish the merchant harshly.

"Birbal," Akbar said, "*justify this decision. The merchant must be punished to set an example. What say you?*"

Birbal looked at Akbar calmly, a quiet seriousness in his eyes. He could have agreed, chosen his words carefully to please the emperor, and kept his position safe. But Birbal's integrity would not allow him to be the voice of injustice.

"*Your Majesty,*" Birbal began gently, "*I understand the need for strong action, but justice is the true foundation of your reign. Punishing an innocent merchant will send the wrong message and shake the people's trust in your court.*"

Akbar raised an eyebrow, intrigued but not yet convinced.

"*The evidence is weak, and the merchant's record shows honesty and fairness. If we punish him without clear proof, what hope will others have of fairness in your kingdom? Will fear rule instead of justice?*"

There was a murmur among the courtiers, some whispered that Birbal was being disrespectful, others admired his courage.

Akbar leaned back, thoughtful. He had tested many advisors before, but Birbal's honesty was different; it was fearless, yet respectful. Instead of anger, a rare smile appeared on the emperor's face.

"*You speak wisely, Birbal,*" Akbar said. "*It takes courage to tell the truth when it's difficult. I respect that. We will reconsider this decision.*"

That day, Birbal's integrity not only saved an innocent man but also strengthened Akbar's reputation as a just ruler. The courtiers who tried to undermine Birbal learned that honesty held a power no flattery or fear could match.

Why does this story matter to you?

In your corporate world, you will face moments where shortcuts, bending rules, or going along with unfair decisions may seem tempting, or even necessary. But like Birbal, your integrity is your true strength. It might feel risky to speak up or stick to your values when the pressure is on, but that's exactly when your character is being built.

Remember, integrity builds trust, the kind that colleagues, managers, and clients respect deeply. And trust? It's the foundation of every successful career.

So when faced with tough choices, channel your inner Birbal. Stand firm, speak truth with grace, and know that while the right path might not always be easy, it's always worth it.

Here are your key learnings.

1. **Ethics and integrity are non-negotiable**
   They are the foundation of your professional reputation.
   Imagine your professional reputation as a sturdy bridge connecting you to opportunities, colleagues, and success. Ethics and integrity are the solid pillars holding up that bridge. No matter how beautifully you decorate the path or how fast you walk across it, if those pillars are weak or shaky, the whole bridge could collapse under pressure.
   You might be tempted to cut corners, use weaker materials or skip inspections, to reach your goals faster. But in the long run, a bridge built on shaky ground won't hold. Similarly, without strong ethics and integrity, your career foundation will crack, and trust will erode.

So, build your bridge with care, honesty, and unwavering principles. That way, your professional journey is not only safe but respected and admired by everyone who crosses it.

2. **Stand your ground**
   Upholding your values might be hard, but it's always worth it.
   Think of yourself as a mighty oak tree standing tall in the middle of a storm. The winds of pressure and temptation howl all around you, urging you to bend, to sway, maybe even to break. But your roots, your values and principles are planted deep and strong in the ground.
   Sure, bending might seem easier in the moment, like avoiding conflict or going along with the crowd. But the oak that stands firm through the storm earns respect and admiration. It doesn't just survive, it thrives.
   Standing like an oak doesn't mean carrying ego or stubbornness, it means holding fast to your ethics with quiet confidence and grace. Upholding your values might feel tough, even lonely sometimes. But just like the oak, your strength and integrity become a beacon others look up to. Standing your ground isn't just about resisting the storm, it's about growing stronger because of it.

3. **Build trust**
   Your integrity will earn you respect and credibility in the long run. Think of trust like a perfect cup of tea brewed slowly and carefully (*as I am writing, I am sitting here, sipping a steaming cup of ginger tea, and that's exactly what inspired me to share this analogy with you*).
   You don't just pour boiling water on tea leaves and expect the best flavour immediately. It takes patience, the right ingredients, and gentle attention over time to get that rich, comforting taste.
   Every time you act with integrity, keeping your promises, being honest, and doing the right thing, you are adding to the steeping process, strengthening the flavour of trust.

If you rush or cut corners, it's like pouring cold water or rushing the brew -the tea ends up weak, bitter, or disappointing. People notice when your actions don't match your words, and their trust in you cools down.

So, build your trust like a slow-brewed tea: with care, patience, and consistency. The reward? A strong, lasting respect and credibility that warms every relationship in your professional journey.

Before we dive into this Self-Evaluation Activity, I want to take a moment to say, this isn't about judgment or perfection. It's about kindness, honesty, and reflection. Think of it as a little heart-to-heart with yourself, a gentle pause to check in on how you are living your values and where you might want to grow.

Over the years, I have found that real growth begins when we look inward with curiosity rather than criticism. So, take a deep breath, be patient with yourself, and get ready to explore where you stand on work ethics and integrity. This is your journey, and every step, no matter how small, matters.

Self-Evaluation Activity

THE INTEGRITY COMPASS

Why does this activity matter?

This exercise helps you stay grounded in your values, even when faced with tough decisions. By creating a decision-making framework, you'll be better equipped to navigate ethical dilemmas and uphold your integrity.

Remember, your reputation is your most valuable asset, protect it at all costs.

What do you need to do?

I hope you continue to either scribble here or write down your response in your notepad.

WORK ETHICS AND INTEGRITY

Step	What to do?	Respond to your questions.
Identify Your Core Values	Think about the values that are most important to you in your professional life. For example: • Honesty • Accountability • Fairness • Respect Write down 3-5 core values that guide your decisions at work.	
Reflect on Past Dilemmas	Think about a time when you faced an ethical dilemma at work. Write down: • What was the situation? • What decision did you make? • How did it align (or not align) with your core values?	
Create a Decision-Making Framework	Based on your core values, create a framework to guide your decisions in ethical dilemmas. For example: • Pause and Reflect: Take a moment to think before making a decision. • Align with Values: Ask yourself, *"Does this decision align with my core values?"* • Consider the Consequences: Think about the short-term and long-term impact of your decision.	

WORK ETHICS AND INTEGRITY

	• Seek Advice: If you're unsure, consult a trusted colleague or mentor.	
Practice with Scenarios	Imagine the following scenarios and apply your decision-making framework: • Your manager asks you to manipulate data to make a project look successful. • A colleague suggests taking credit for someone else's work to impress the boss. • You notice a team member consistently cutting corners, but no one else seems to care. Write down how you would handle each situation based on your core values.	
Commit to Your Values	Finally, write down a commitment to yourself. For example: • *"I will always prioritize honesty and transparency in my work."* • *"I will stand by my values, even when it's difficult."* • *"I will seek advice when faced with ethical dilemmas."*	

As you complete this self-evaluation, take a moment to reflect deeply on the essence of integrity. It's often said that integrity is what you do when nobody is watching, and that's because it truly reveals the core of your character. It's not just about following rules or meeting expectations; it's about cultivating an attitude that consistently chooses honesty, fairness, and ethical behaviour, even in the smallest moments.

WORK ETHICS AND INTEGRITY

Building a reputation grounded in integrity is a journey, a journey that unfolds over years of deliberate choices, trust earned, and respect gained. It requires patience and a steadfast commitment to your values, especially when the easier path might tempt you to compromise.

But here's the truth: while it takes time to build this foundation, it can be shattered in an instant by a single careless act or moment of weakness.

This delicate balance places a profound responsibility in your hands. You are the guardian of your own reputation, and every decision shapes the story people will tell about you. So, as you move forward, ask yourself,

"how will you act when no one's watching"?

"What kind of professional, and more importantly, what kind of person do you want to be"?

Let this awareness be your compass, guiding you to consistently choose integrity in every step you take.

Leverage Birbal's Wisdom in Action

As we wrap up this chapter, let's take a moment to reflect on Birbal's timeless example. In Akbar's court, Birbal wasn't just admired for his wit or intelligence, he was revered because he stood firm on his principles, even when it wasn't easy. His unwavering integrity became the foundation of his influence and respect, proving that true success is built not just on what you achieve, but on how you achieve it.

So, here's something to ponder:

When faced with tough choices, will you stand by your values, even if it means standing alone?

How do you want others to remember you, not just as a skilled professional, but as a person of character?

What small daily actions can you take to strengthen your own foundation of ethics and integrity?

> Remember, building a career like Birbal's isn't about shortcuts or compromises. It's about showing up authentically, standing your ground with grace, and letting your integrity light the path ahead. Your journey may have challenges, but it will also have the kind of respect and trust that lasts a lifetime.
> *What will your legacy be?*

Before we close this chapter, here's one of my favourite quotes on integrity that has guided me through my career. You may like it too.

> **"IN LOOKING FOR PEOPLE TO HIRE, YOU LOOK FOR THREE QUALITIES: INTEGRITY, INTELLIGENCE, AND ENERGY. AND IF THEY DON'T HAVE THE FIRST, THE OTHER TWO WILL KILL YOU."**
> **— WARREN BUFFETT**

CHAPTER 6
BUILDING YOUR PERSONAL BRAND
BE MEMORABLE

Alright, let's talk about something that's going to set you apart in the corporate world:

<u>YOUR PERSONAL BRAND</u>

Picture this.

Imagine Aman, a young professional who has just started his first job at a big company. Like most of us, Aman was eager to prove himself. He worked hard, completed his tasks on time, and kept his head down. But he noticed something curious: despite all his effort, people rarely called on him for projects or important meetings. It was as if he was invisible in the crowd.

One day, during a team discussion, a colleague said, *"Hey Aman, could you help with the quarterly reports? You're great with numbers."* Aman was surprised, he hadn't realized that his work was being noticed for that specific skill. That moment sparked something in him. He realized he already had a personal brand: *"the numbers guy."* But it wasn't intentional, it was just the way people perceived him based on his consistent work.

From then on, Aman decided to be more deliberate. He started sharing insights during meetings, offering help beyond his tasks, and making sure his contributions were visible, not in a bragging way, but authentically. Slowly, his personal brand grew from *"just the numbers guy"* to *"the reliable problem solver."* People began to seek his advice, and new opportunities started knocking on his door.

BUILDING YOUR PERSONAL BRAND

Here's the thing: like Aman, you already have a personal brand. It's shaped by how you show up, what you do, and what you communicate, whether you mean to or not. The real power lies in taking control of that story. So, before you wonder what others think of you, ask yourself: *What story do you want them to tell? And how will you shape it, step by step, day by day?*

That's what building your personal brand is all about. Not a flashy makeover, but a genuine, consistent reflection of who you are and the value you bring. Ready to explore how you can craft that story? Let's dive in.

Let's Learn from Birbal's Life Event

In the royal court of Emperor Akbar, wisdom was abundant, but so were challenges, politics, and a fair share of drama. Among all the courtiers, one man stood apart, not just because of his clever mind, but because of how he used it. That man was Birbal.

Now, Birbal wasn't just Akbar's wise advisor who came up with clever riddles to amuse the emperor. No, Birbal had a personal brand long before the phrase was even invented. It was a brand built on trust, consistency, and a dash of cheeky wit that made him both respected and beloved.

Here's the thing: Birbal could have been just another smart guy in the court. There were plenty of scholars and advisors, each eager to impress the emperor. But what made Birbal different was how he showed up every day. He wasn't just solving puzzles or telling jokes for fun; he was solving real problems, big and small, in ways that made everyone's life easier - even the Emperor's.

Take the famous story when Akbar once challenged Birbal with a question that seemed impossible: *"Birbal, how can you find the sharpest sword in the kingdom without testing every single one?"*

The other courtiers scrambled to suggest complicated methods, but Birbal simply walked to the armoury, tapped each sword lightly, and then asked the guards to fetch one in particular. It turned out that his 'test' was his keen observation and experience, something only he had honed over time.

What does this teach us?

Birbal's brand was not about showing off his intelligence but about using it effectively. He was reliable, consistent, and practical. People knew that when Birbal spoke, he had thought things through, and his advice wasn't just clever, it worked.

Even more importantly, Birbal stayed true to his values. He didn't twist the truth to please the emperor; he told him what he needed to hear, even if it was uncomfortable. That took courage and integrity, and that's why Akbar trusted him like no other. Birbal's brand was authentic, it was built on who he really was, not a mask he wore to fit in.

Now, think about your own personal brand in the corporate world. Are you like Birbal, the person who quietly but consistently gets things done, speaks up when it matters, and stays true to your values? Or are you letting others shape your story for you?

Birbal's journey reminds us that building your brand isn't about loud applause or flashy titles. It's about the everyday choices you make, the way you handle challenges, and the kind of reputation you nurture over time. Like Birbal, your wisdom and integrity become your signature, something people remember long after you leave the room.

So, the next time you wonder if your work is noticed, remember Birbal. He didn't need to shout to be heard. He simply showed up, day after day, with his authentic self and sharp mind, and that made all the difference.

Here are your key learnings.

1. **Your personal brand is your reputation**
   It's what people say about you when you are not in the room.

Imagine you are at a party, and you have just stepped out of the room for a moment. Now, picture the people still there quietly chatting about you, not just what you said or did while you were there, but who you are in their eyes. That's your personal brand in action.

Your personal brand is like an invisible storyteller, weaving tales about you when you are not around. It's the reputation that travels ahead of you, shaping how people think, feel, and decide whether they want to work with you, trust you, or seek your advice.

Just like a good story spreads and sticks in people's minds, your personal brand sticks because of the impressions you leave behind, your work, your attitude, your values, and even how you treat others.

So, the big question is: *What kind of story do you want people to tell when you are not in the room?*

2. **Be intentional**

    Identify your strengths and align them with what your organization values.

    Imagine your personal brand like a playlist you create on your favourite music app. You have countless songs (your skills and strengths) to choose from, but you want your playlist to send a clear vibe, whether it's upbeat, chill, or inspiring.

    Being intentional means carefully selecting tracks that fit the mood you want to set and that resonate with your listeners, just like aligning your strengths with what your organization values. If your playlist is all over the place, your audience might get confused or lose interest.

    But when your playlist has a consistent style and flow, people recognize it, remember it, and come back for more. That's exactly how a strong personal brand works, it reflects who you are and what you bring, in a way that connects with your professional world.

    So, what kind of playlist are you curating with your personal brand?

BUILDING YOUR PERSONAL BRAND

Before we jump into the self-evaluation, let me share a quick confession: I once thought "personal branding" was just a fancy buzzword people used on LinkedIn while posing with their coffee mugs. You know the kind, filter on, hashtag ready, and a caption like "Hustle, grind, repeat."

But the truth hit me during a performance review when my manager said, *"You are reliable, but I am not exactly sure what your superpower is."* That stung. Because deep down, I knew I was doing meaningful work, but I hadn't been intentional about how others perceived it.

That's when I realized: your personal brand isn't built by accident. It's built by design. It's not about being flashy or fake, it's about being you, consistently and clearly, in a way that aligns with what your team and organization need.

So, let's pause here and take a closer look at how you are shaping your brand. Grab a pen, a cup of *chai* (or coffee, no judgment), and let's get to know the most important brand you will ever manage - YOURS.

Self-Evaluation Activity

THE PERSONAL BRAND BLUEPRINT

Why does this activity matter?

This exercise helps you take control of your personal brand and ensure it aligns with your goals and values. By being intentional about how you present yourself, you can build a reputation that opens doors for your career.

Remember, your personal brand is your professional legacy - make it count.

What do you need to do?

While enjoying your tea and coffee introspect on these action item.

BUILDING YOUR PERSONAL BRAND

Step	What to do?	Respond to your questions.
Identify Your Strengths	Think about what you are really good at. For example: • *Are you a great problem-solver?* • *Do you have excellent communication skills?* • *Are you known for your creativity or attention to detail?* Write down 3-5 strengths that define you professionally.	
Define Your Unique Value Proposition	Your Unique Value Proposition (UVP) is what sets you apart from others. Ask yourself: • *What do I do better than anyone else?* • *What value do I bring to my team or organization?* • *How do I want to be perceived by others?* Write a short statement that summarizes your UVP. For example: • *"I'm the go-to person for turning complex data into actionable insights."* • *"I bring creativity and innovation to every project I work on."*	

Align with Organizational Values	Think about what your organization values most. For example: • *Does it prioritize innovation, collaboration, or customer focus?* • *How can your strengths align with these values?* Write down 2-3 ways you can showcase your strengths in a way that aligns with your organization's values.	
Create a Visibility Plan	Building your personal brand isn't just about doing great work, it's about making sure others see it. Write down 2-3 actions you can take to increase your visibility. For example: • Volunteer to lead a high-profile project. • Share your achievements in team meetings or through email updates. • Network with colleagues in other departments to expand your influence.	
Reflect and Refine	After a month, revisit your personal brand blueprint and reflect: • *Have you been consistent in showcasing your strengths?* • *How have others responded to your efforts?* • *Are there any adjustments you need to make?*	

BUILDING YOUR PERSONAL BRAND

So, how did that self-reflection feels? Eye-opening? Slightly awkward? Empowering? Maybe all of the above?

Here's the thing: building your personal brand isn't about copying someone else's brilliance. It's about discovering your own. Sure, it's easy to fall into the trap of mimicking a leader you admire or talking like that confident colleague who always seems to have the right words. But remember, what makes them memorable is their authenticity.

You are not here to be a second version of someone else. You are here to be the first and only version of you.

Let your work speak for itself, yes, but let you shine through it. Your quirks, your values, your strengths, that's your brand. And it's powerful, especially when it comes from a place of self-awareness and purpose.

So ask yourself:

- *Am I letting people see the real me?*
- *Does my brand reflect who I truly am and what I stand for?*
- *Am I evolving as I grow, both personally and professionally?*

Keep showing up with intention. Keep refining. Keep being you, because the world doesn't need another carbon copy. It needs your original voice.

Leverage Birbal's Wisdom in Action

Birbal's Final Nudge: The Signature You Leave Behind

In the grand court of Akbar, Birbal didn't announce his brilliance with trumpets. He didn't chase applause or decorate his title with borrowed feathers. He simply showed up, again and again, with sharp thinking, a sense of humor, and a heart full of purpose.

That was his brand.

And it wasn't accidental, it was built, one story at a time, one honest word at a time, one fearless truth at a time.

BUILDING YOUR PERSONAL BRAND

> Now think about your workplace as your own little court. You don't need to be the loudest or flashiest. Be like Birbal, let your strengths speak, let your consistency echo, and let your values shine through the choices you make. Your personal brand isn't just about your skillset - it's about the signature you leave behind in every meeting, email, project, or problem solved.
>
> So, dear reader, what tale will your brand tell when you're not in the room? Whatever it is, make it unmistakably yours. Because like Birbal, the goal isn't just to be remembered. The goal is to be remembered for the right reasons.

One quote that has stayed with me over the years and has quietly influenced how I carry myself at work is by Jeff Bezos, the founder of Amazon. It's one of my all-time favourite quotes, and I hope it stays with you too, like a quiet voice nudging you to show up with authenticity, every single day.

Simple. Honest. Powerful.

> "YOUR BRAND IS WHAT PEOPLE SAY ABOUT YOU WHEN YOU'RE NOT IN THE ROOM."
> — JEFF BEZOS

CHAPTER 7
DOING THE RIGHT THINGS
VERSUS. DOING THINGS RIGHT

Let's talk about a trap that so many of us fall into:

<u>WORKING HARD BUT NOT REALLY GETTING ANYWHERE</u>

"Busy doesn't always mean productive, sometimes it just means... well, busy."

Let me ask you a few questions.

Have you ever rearranged your desk for 45 minutes just to mentally prepare to start working?

Have you ever spent an hour color-coding an Excel sheet that no one asked for?

Or proudly finished every item on your to-do list, only to realize none of it really mattered?

Welcome to the classic productivity paradox: You are hustling like a boss, but somehow, the needle doesn't move. You are doing things right, efficiently, neatly, even impressively, but are you doing the right things?

Let's pause and chew on that (*preferably with a cookie and some tea*).

There's a huge difference between being efficient and being effective. Efficiency is completing a task quickly and correctly. Effectiveness is choosing the right task in the first place. One keeps you busy, the other propels you forward.

DOING THE RIGHT THINGS

So here's the uncomfortable truth: You could be the most organized, punctual, detail-oriented employee in your team, and still be invisible if your energy is spent on things that don't align with your goals or your team's priorities.

The corporate world doesn't reward effort alone; it rewards impact.

And impact comes when you combine smart choices with smart execution.

It's not just about sharpening the knife; it's about making sure you are cutting the right tree.

So, as we dive into this chapter, think about this:

Are you sprinting on a treadmill or walking towards a meaningful destination?

Let's Learn from Birbal's Life Event

One fine morning in the Mughal court, Emperor Akbar was unusually restless. A foreign ambassador had presented him with what he claimed was a priceless feather from a mythical bird. The court buzzed with curiosity, and ministers debated its origins, its rarity, and how best to display it.

The royal treasurer proposed building a golden case for it. The artists suggested painting a giant mural in its honour. The royal poet even started composing verses about its elegance.

And where was Birbal in all this? Quiet. Observing. Thinking.

When Akbar finally turned to him and asked, *"Birbal, what do you think we should do with this miraculous feather?"*

Birbal, in his usual calm tone, replied, *"Jahapanah, may I ask, what value does a feather hold if we do not know the bird it came from?"*

Silence. You could hear the collective gasp of the court.

He continued, *"We are about to spend precious time and royal funds glorifying something without knowing if it truly holds worth. Instead, shouldn't we focus on the real matters of the kingdom, ones that affect your people, your trade, your peace?"*

Akbar chuckled. *"As always, Birbal, you fly straight to the point."*

And just like that, the feather was shelved, the gold saved, and the emperor's attention redirected to urgent matters like water scarcity in a nearby province.

Birbal didn't just solve riddles; he solved priorities.

He didn't waste time doing unimportant things with flair, he focused on what truly mattered.

In today's world, we often spend energy perfecting presentations no one reads, beautifying reports that have no impact, and attending meetings that don't need us.

Birbal reminds us: doing things right is good, but doing the right things is game-changing.

Here are your key learnings.

1. **Focus on high-impact activities**
   Prioritize tasks that align with your goals and your organization's priorities.
   Imagine a tiny coastal town that depends on a lighthouse to guide ships safely through stormy nights.
   The lighthouse keeper, Mr. Sen, was known for being incredibly meticulous. He polished the brass fixtures daily, dusted every corner, even rearranged the books in the keeper's quarters alphabetically. Everything was spotless.
   But one night, during a particularly fierce storm, the light in the tower flickered, and went out.

DOING THE RIGHT THINGS

In all his dedication to maintaining the appearance of the lighthouse, Mr. Sen had overlooked the most crucial task: refuelling the light.

That night, a ship narrowly missed crashing into the rocks, not because the keeper wasn't working hard, but because he wasn't focusing on the one task that mattered the most.

In the corporate world, we often become Mr. Sen, busy polishing our to-do lists, attending meetings, replying to every email, feeling productive. But the real question is: *Are we keeping the light on?*

High-impact work isn't about how much you do, it's about what you choose to do.

Pause and Reflect:

- *Are you spending your energy polishing tasks that just make you look busy?*
- *Which activities in your role are the light, the ones that truly drive results or visibility?*
- *If you stopped doing 30% of your routine work, would anyone notice, or would it finally give you space to focus on what truly matters?*

Choose wisely. The ships are counting on you.

2. **Learn to say no**

    Don't let low-priority tasks distract you from what's truly important.

    Imagine you are at a grand buffet. The star of the menu? Your favourite - rich, aromatic Hyderabadi biryani. But as you pick up your plate and move down the line, someone offers you a spoonful of bland boiled veggies. (*To all my fellow vegetarians, don't get me wrong, I absolutely love my veggies, but let's be honest, biryani has my whole heart, every single time.*)

    You smile politely and say '*yes*'. Then someone adds plain white rice. Then a helping of soggy salad. A few bites later, your plate is full, but there's no space left for the biryani.

    Frustrating, right?

    Now pause.

DOING THE RIGHT THINGS

That plate is your time at work.

The biryani? That's your high-impact, meaningful work. The kind that moves the needle and brings visibility. But every time you say "yes" to low-priority, non-value-adding tasks just to be helpful or liked, you are filling your plate with boiled distractions.

Saying yes to everything is not kindness, it's mismanagement.

Now, don't get me wrong, being a team player matters. But so does protecting your time for what truly deserves it.

Now, Ask Yourself:

- *Is your workplace plate full of biryani or bland obligations?*
- *Are you accepting every task to avoid discomfort, or because it really aligns with your goals?*
- *What's one task this week you can politely decline, or delegate, so you can make room for what matters?*

Remember, saying "no" doesn't have to sound rude.

Try:

"This looks interesting, but I'm currently focused on [your priority task]. Can we revisit this later?"

"Happy to support, could we reassign this so I can give it the attention it deserves?"

Remember, it's your plate. Fill it wisely.

I am being completely honest, learning to say "no" didn't come easy to me. In the early years of my career, I said yes to almost everything, every task, every request, every last-minute *"can you help with this?"* Not because I wanted to impress, but because I genuinely believed that saying yes was the right thing to do.

I wore my busyness like a badge of honour, until I realized I was drowning in to-do lists with little to show for it in terms of impact. It hit me one day, painfully, that despite doing tons of work, not much of it truly moved the needle. My calendar was full, but my value didn't feel visible. That's when I slowly started practicing the art of saying no, not out of arrogance, but out of clarity.

Saying no to low-priority noise allowed me to say a big, focused YES to the work that mattered. It saved my sanity and my credibility.

So before you dive into this self-evaluation, take a breath, reflect, and remember: boundaries aren't barriers, they are bridges to better outcomes.

Self-Evaluation Activity

THE PRIORITY MATRIX

Why does this activity matter?

This activity will help you identify and focus on high-impact activities.

This exercise helps you focus on what truly matters, rather than getting bogged down in busywork. By prioritizing high-impact activities, you will not only achieve more but also make a bigger impact on your career and your organization.

It is not about how much you do, it's about how much you accomplish.

What do you need to do?

Grab a notebook or open that forever-minimized MS Word document, we both know it's hiding somewhere on your desktop.

Step	What to do?	Respond to your questions.
List Your Tasks	Think about everything on your to-do list. Write down all the tasks you need to complete, both big and small. For example: • Finish the quarterly report. • Respond to emails. • Attend team meetings.	

	• Work on the new marketing strategy.	
Categorize Your Tasks	Using the Eisenhower Matrix, categorize your tasks into four quadrants: • Urgent and Important: Tasks that need immediate attention and have a big impact (For example: finishing a project deadline). • Not Urgent but Important: Tasks that are important but don't need immediate attention (For example: planning for a future project). • Urgent but Not Important: Tasks that need immediate attention but don't have a big impact (For example: responding to certain emails). • Not Urgent and Not Important: Tasks that are neither urgent nor important (For example: browsing social media).	
Prioritize High-Impact Activities	Focus on the tasks in the first two quadrants (Urgent and Important, Not Urgent but Important). These are the tasks that will have the biggest impact on your goals and your organization's priorities. For example: • If you are working on a high-profile project, prioritize tasks that move it forward. • If you are planning for a future initiative, allocate time to strategize and prepare.	
Delegate or Eliminate	For tasks in the last two quadrants (Urgent but Not Important, Not Urgent and Not Important), consider:	

Low-Impact Activities	• Delegating them to someone else (For example: ask a colleague to handle certain emails). • Eliminating them altogether (For example: reduce time spent on non-essential meetings).	
Create a Focus Plan	Based on your Priority Matrix, write down a plan for the week. For example: • *"I will spend 80% of my time on high-impact activities like finishing the quarterly report and planning the new marketing strategy."* • *"I will delegate low-priority tasks like responding to routine emails."* • *"I will eliminate distractions like unnecessary meetings and social media browsing."*	

So, *how did that feel? A little eye-opening? A bit liberating? Maybe even a tad uncomfortable?* That's a good sign. You just took a meaningful pause to reflect, not on how busy you are, but on how wisely your time and energy are spent.

Remember this: If everything is marked as a priority, then truly, nothing is. Period.

It's easy to get swept up in the whirlwind of tasks, requests, and emails flying at you from all directions. But growth lies in clarity. Progress begins when you can confidently say, *"This matters right now, and that can wait."*

Your value at work isn't measured by how much you juggle, it's by how well you choose what to catch. So, take this insight forward. Revisit your goals, realign your energy, and most importantly, give yourself permission to focus on what truly matters.

Because doing the right things, even imperfectly, beats doing everything perfectly.

Now go be that person who not only gets things done, but gets the right things done.

> **Leverage Birbal's Wisdom in Action**
>
> If Birbal were in the modern workplace, you would probably find him sipping masala chai in a meeting room, calmly solving problems while everyone else is frantically color-coding spreadsheets that no one reads.
>
> Why? Because Birbal knew the secret, doing the right things trumps doing all the things right.
>
> When faced with chaos, he didn't rush to complete every task. He chose the smartest one. While others polished pebbles, Birbal picked diamonds. And that, my friend, is how legends are made.
>
> So the next time you are tempted to say yes to everything, ask yourself: *Is this a royal problem or just a royal distraction?*
>
> Focus like Birbal. Act with intention. And never forget, you are not here to be the busiest in the room, you are here to be the wisest.
>
> Now go on, make your choices count, the empire is watching!

Before we wrap up, here's something I hold close to my heart, one of my favourite quotes about doing the right things. This quote always reminds me that being busy doesn't mean we are moving forward. Like Birbal, I have learnt that focus and purpose are everything.

So as you build your career, ask yourself:

Are you just doing things right, or are you doing the right things? Because that small shift can change everything.

Here's to working smarter, not just harder, Birbal style.

"IT IS NOT ENOUGH TO BE BUSY; SO ARE THE ANTS. THE QUESTION IS: WHAT ARE WE BUSY ABOUT?"
— HENRY DAVID

CHAPTER 8
PATIENCE AND PROMOTIONS
THE LONG GAME

Let's talk about something that needs our dedicated attention in the corporate world:

PATIENCE

Let me tell you about Ravi. He joined a large corporate firm fresh out of college, full of enthusiasm and ready to conquer the world. Like many of us, Ravi believed hard work would guarantee quick promotions. So, he worked tirelessly, took on extra projects, stayed late to help teammates, and always delivered his best. Yet, year after year, the promotion he expected remained elusive.

Frustrated, Ravi once confided in his mentor, *"I have been doing everything right, but it feels like I am stuck in the slow lane. Why does success seem to favour others who don't even try as hard?"*

His mentor smiled and said, *"Ravi, success is not a vending machine where you put in coins and get a snack immediately. It's more like growing a mango tree. You plant the seed, water it patiently, and wait through the seasons. Some years, you see no fruit at all. But when the tree finally bears fruit, it's sweeter than you could have imagined."*

That conversation changed Ravi's perspective. He stopped chasing instant results and focused on steady growth, learning, and building relationships. And over time, the recognition and promotions started coming, not because he rushed, but because he mastered the art of patience.

Ravi's story reminds us that careers aren't sprint races; they are marathons. Promotions don't always come when we want, but when the time is right, they arrive as a reward for consistent effort and unwavering patience.

So, if you feel stuck or overlooked, remember: just like a fruit tree, your growth needs time. Keep nurturing your skills, stay patient, and trust the process. The long game is where the real success lies.

Let's Learn from Birbal's Life Event

Long before Birbal became Akbar's most trusted advisor, he was just another face in the crowd at the royal court. Witty, yes. Observant, undoubtedly. But in *durbar* full of scholars, poets, and seasoned ministers, Birbal was still just finding his ground.

One hot afternoon, Emperor Akbar summoned his courtiers to discuss a pressing matter, a province under the empire was facing rebellion. Each minister offered complex strategies, full of maps and military jargon. Birbal, standing quietly at the edge, chose not to speak. Akbar noticed his silence.

"*You have nothing to say, Birbal?*" Akbar asked, slightly amused.

"*I do, Your Majesty,*" Birbal replied calmly. "*But may I speak once the noise settles?*"

There was laughter in the court. Some smirked, thinking he had no plan at all. But Akbar, curious, nodded.

Days passed. The rebellion fizzled out on its own, not through battle, but because the local leaders couldn't unite. Akbar called Birbal once again.

"*Tell me now, why didn't you speak that day?*"

Birbal smiled. "*Because wisdom, like mangoes, must ripen before it's shared. I knew the problem wasn't the province, it was their egos. They would destroy themselves without a single sword drawn. Sometimes, the right move is waiting.*"

PATIENCE AND PROMOTIONS

From that day on, Akbar began to see Birbal in a different light. Not because he was loud, or eager to impress, but because he knew when to act, and more importantly, when to hold back.

Yet even after that, it wasn't immediate. Birbal faced envy, subtle exclusions from court decisions, and occasional public ridicule from senior ministers who couldn't understand his calm confidence. But he never retaliated or complained. He kept showing up, kept observing, and when the time was right, he spoke, always with depth, always with wit, and always with grace.

One day, when the empire faced a financial conundrum, Birbal proposed a simple but genius system to reorganize tax collection. The revenue stabilized, the people were relieved, and Akbar, impressed beyond measure, stood up in court and declared:

"From today, Birbal is not just my advisor, he is my mirror. He shows me the truth, even when I do not want to see it."

Why This Still Matters Today?

Birbal didn't chase power. He cultivated trust. He didn't grab the spotlight. He waited until his light was undeniable.

In today's fast-paced work culture, we are tempted to want everything now - promotions, recognition, influence. But as Birbal showed, the real currency is consistency. It's not the loudest voice that's heard the longest; it's the wisest one that echoes through time.

So if you are feeling overlooked, or your efforts seem to go unnoticed, channel your inner Birbal. Stay the course. Build your value patiently. Don't confuse speed with progress. Because when the moment comes, and it will, you won't just be ready. You will be irreplaceable.

Here are your key learnings.

1. **Patience is a virtue**
   Promotions and rewards take time, so don't expect instant results. Your career is like an avocado!

Imagine you are craving guacamole. You spot the perfect avocado at the store, shiny, promising, full of potential. You bring it home, eager to slice it open, but wait, it's still hard as a rock. You nudge it every hour.

You Google hacks. You even consider microwaving it (*Please don't*).

But the truth is, no matter how many life hacks you try, an avocado ripens when it's ready, not a moment before.

Your career? It's the same.

You might be putting in the hours, learning the tools, showing up, and crushing your goals, but promotions won't happen just because you are eager. Like the avocado, you need the right time, right environment, and a bit of natural ripening. The result? Worth it.

A beautifully ripe avocado, or a well-earned promotion, is not just satisfying, it's sustainable.

So, next time you feel like things aren't moving fast enough, remember: even guacamole takes patience. Don't rush it. Trust the process. Your moment will come, and when it does, it will be chef's kiss perfect.

2. **Focus on the long game**

    Keep learning, growing, and delivering great work, even if it feels like no one's noticing.

    Ever tried doing a giant 1000-piece puzzle without the picture on the box? It's chaotic at first. You don't know where anything fits. You keep matching pieces, trying patterns, flipping colours, and it feels like nothing's working.

    That's what the early years of a career feel like sometimes.

    You are learning new skills, taking on projects, staying late, helping others, and wondering, "*Is anyone even noticing this*?"

    But here's the truth: just like a puzzle, every piece you are placing now, every skill, every success, every little win, is adding to the bigger picture. You just can't see it yet.

And suddenly, one day, something clicks. The edges start forming. The bigger picture begins to take shape. And that's when others start seeing the masterpiece you have been quietly working on.

So, keep going. Keep learning, keep contributing, and trust that every piece counts. The long game is slow, but it's how masterpieces are built.

3. **Be ready for opportunities**

   When the time is right, make sure you are prepared to seize the moment.

   Imagine you are at an open mic night. You are sitting in the crowd, watching others perform, some great, some.... well, trying. You have got your piece ready, just in case, but you are not on the list. You wait, sip your beverage, and cheer others on.

   Then suddenly, the host says, *"Anyone else want to come up and give it a shot?"*

   Here's the catch: if your guitar is still in its case, or your notes are scattered in your bag, that moment slips away.

   That's how opportunities work in real life too.

   They don't always come with a formal invite or perfect timing. Sometimes they show up on a random Tuesday afternoon in a hallway conversation or a surprise vacancy.

   The question is, are you ready to walk up and own the mic?

   So keep refining your skills, keep your tools sharp, and stay show-ready, because when the spotlight finds you, you would want to be the one who steps up and delivers a performance worth remembering.

Before we dive into the self-evaluation, let's hit pause for a second.

Think of this as a gentle coffee or tea break for your career, a moment to breathe, reflect, and check in with yourself. I know the waiting game for recognition can feel like watching paint dry while juggling ten other tasks, but here's a little secret: how you use the "waiting" phase says a lot about your growth mindset.

So let's turn inward for a bit. No rush, no judgment, just you and your thoughts. Grab your journal, open that Google Doc, or scribble on a napkin if that's your jam. Reflect on where you are, where you want to be, and how you have handled the stretch between the two.

Ready? Let's get a little real and a little reflective.

Self-Evaluation Activity

THE PATIENCE AND PERSISTENCE PLAN

Why does this activity matter?

This activity helps you stay focused and motivated, even when progress feels slow. By setting clear goals, identifying gaps, and creating a plan, you will be better prepared to seize opportunities when they arise.

Remember, patience isn't about waiting, it's about working consistently toward your goals, even when the results aren't immediate.

Time to action!

Step	What to do?	Respond to your questions.
Reflect on Your Career Goals	Think about where you want to be in your career. Write down: • What position or role are you aiming for? • What skills or experiences do you need to get there? • What's your timeline for achieving these goals?	
Identify Your Strengths and Gaps	Take stock of where you are right now. Write down: • What are your current strengths (For example: technical skills, leadership abilities)? • What gaps do you need to fill (For example: certifications, networking, experience)?	
Create a Learning and Development Plan	Based on your reflections, write down 2-3 actionable steps to bridge the gaps. For example: • *"I will take a course on project management to strengthen my skills."* • *"I will seek mentorship from a senior leader in my organization."*	

		• "I will volunteer for cross-functional projects to gain broader experience."	
Track Your Progress	Create a system to track your progress over time. For example: • Keep a journal of your achievements and lessons learned. • Set quarterly check-ins to review your goals and adjust your plan as needed.		
Celebrate Small Wins	While you are waiting for the big milestones, don't forget to celebrate the small wins along the way. For example: • "I successfully led a team meeting, go me!" • "I received positive feedback from my manager, time to treat myself!"		

Alright, deep breath... and exhale. You just took a big, bold step toward understanding the art of playing the long game.

And here's the golden nugget to carry forward: Patience isn't you lounging around, sipping *chai*, waiting for your boss to notice your genius. Nope. It's you showing up, putting in the reps, staying sharp, and trusting that consistency beats chaos - every time.

Think of your career less like popcorn in a microwave and more like *dum biryani*. Slow, steady, layered with effort, and oh-so-worth-it when it's ready. You can't rush a masterpiece. You are marinating in experience right now, and when the time's right - boom, the lid lifts, and opportunity smells the delicious effort you have put in.

So, as you wrap this up, pat yourself on the back. You are not lost; you are just simmering. And when the moment comes, you will be spicy, seasoned, and ready to serve.

Now go on, stay patient, stay delicious.

Leverage Birbal's Wisdom in Action

In the quiet corridors of Akbar's court, Birbal didn't rush. He didn't chase praise or pace impatiently for promotions. He listened, he learnt, he solved what mattered, and above all, he trusted the rhythm of time.

So, my adorable readers, let Birbal's way be your compass.

Like Birbal, keep your heart steady, your mind sharp, and your spirit light. Your moment will arrive, not as a surprise, but as a result of the roots you have been watering all along. Be patient. Be ready. And never forget - some of the finest stories take time to unfold.

There's one quote that has anchored me through all the "*not yets*" and "*just wait a little longer*" moments in my career.

It reminds me that while the wait may test every fibre of your being, what you are building is worth it. Every pause, every delay, every unnoticed effort, it's all part of a bigger, richer story that's still unfolding.

So, if you are waiting, don't worry. You are not standing still. You are simply ripening.

> "PATIENCE IS BITTER, BUT ITS FRUIT IS SWEET."
> — ARISTOTLE

CHAPTER 9
CORPORATE CULTURE
ADAPTING AND THRIVING

Let's talk about something that can make or break your career:

CORPORATE CULTURE

What do mood playlists, trending reels, and corporate culture have in common?

You don't always know who created them or why they are trending, but you instantly feel the vibe, and you had better adjust your rhythm if you want to fit in.

Seriously, though, have you ever walked into a Zoom call and immediately sensed the vibe?

Like, *"Whoa, this place is chill,"* or *"Okay... are we allowed to blink here?"*

That, my friend, is corporate culture!

The invisible energy field that governs how people behave, communicate, and make decisions in a workplace.

Now here's the kicker:

If you are a Gen Z or Alpha, you have grown up swiping through life, curating your vibe, and expressing your opinions in DMs, reels, and emojis.

And suddenly...

You are expected to decode an office where your manager still uses "Regards" in emails like it's 2007 and calls Microsoft Teams "The Teams."

Welcome to the real-time challenge of adapting to a workplace where your leaders might be Millennials or even Boomers. They may not speak your digital dialect, but they do hold the playbook for success in that organization. And trust me, it's not pinned on the notice board.

So let's pause for a quick pulse check:

Are you trying to be your authentic self but feel like you are in a costume party no one told you about?

Do you ever wonder why some colleagues seem to "get it" and others are constantly playing catch-up?

Have you noticed how some teams are all about open banter, while others treat small talk like a felony?

If any of that rings true, you are not alone.

Every company has a culture, some are built on brainstorming and beanbags, others on hierarchy and hush-hush meetings.

But here's the truth bomb:

Adapting doesn't mean losing yourself. It means learning the unspoken rules, observing the rhythm, and slowly figuring out how to dance to the beat without losing your groove.

Let's crack the culture code together.

Let's Learn from Birbal's Life Event

Let's rewind to a time before Zoom calls, Teams chat or even emails, back to the grand Mughal court of Emperor Akbar.

Now, imagine this as the ultimate workplace: political undertones, powerful personalities, shifting loyalties, and zero HR policies. This wasn't your average 9-to-5 gig. But right in the middle of it all stood Birbal a- quick-witted, observant, and deeply self-aware.

Birbal didn't walk into the court trying to overhaul how things worked. He didn't complain about the vibe, or try to prove he was the smartest person in the room (even though he often was). Instead, he watched. He listened. He learnt the rhythms of Akbar's court, the moods, the hierarchies, the spoken and unspoken rules. And then, like a master strategist, he began weaving his wisdom into the fabric of that culture.

But here's the real magic: Birbal never lost his essence. He stayed rooted in his values, even while adapting to the world around him. And that's why he thrived, not because he changed the system, but because he learnt how to navigate it without losing himself.

That's exactly what the modern workplace needs from you. Culture may not come with a manual, but with a little Birbal-like wisdom, you can find your way.

Here are your key learnings.

1. **Corporate culture is powerful**
   It shapes how people behave, communicate, and make decisions.
   Think of corporate culture like your phone's operating system (iOS or Android). It's not always visible on the surface, but it controls everything, how apps behave, how notifications show up, even how fast your phone responds.
   Now, imagine trying to run an iOS app on an Android phone. It won't work the way it's supposed to. That's exactly what happens when you try to work in a company without understanding its culture. You might have all the right skills, but if you are not synced with the environment, your effectiveness takes a hit.
   Your colleagues might seem super formal in emails while you are dropping emojis. Or maybe decision-making feels like a long winding road while you are used to quick polls on Instagram stories.

Corporate culture is the background code, once you understand it, you can flow smoother, communicate better, and make more impact.

2. **Adaptation is key**
   Understanding and aligning with your organization's culture is crucial for success.
   Think of Yourself as a Spotify Playlist.
   Imagine walking into a room where everyone's vibing to classical music, but your personal playlist is full of EDM drops and K-pop beats. If you blast your playlist at full volume without reading the room, you might get some side-eyes, even if your music is lit.
   Now, think of your professional identity as a Spotify playlist. Your values, personality, and strengths are your core tracks. But when you enter a new company. a new "room", you need to adjust your playlist just enough to match the mood without losing your signature vibe.
   This doesn't mean changing who you are. It means blending your style with the organization's tone, rhythm, and tempo. Maybe it's toning down the bass during meetings or remixing your communication style for different stakeholders.
   The best playlists are the ones that fit the moment and leave a lasting impression. So while staying true to yourself, learn the organization's beat, its decision-making pace, its communication norms, even its dress code and values. Sync your tempo with theirs. Because in the corporate world, those who adapt, not just the loudest tracks, get played on repeat.

Let's pause for a beat.

You have probably been navigating a lot, new job, new team, new lingo (what even is "circle back or keep me posted"?). And while you are scrolling through endless feeds and jumping between group chats and meetings, there's one thing that doesn't come with push notifications: self-awareness.

So before we jump into this self-evaluation, ask yourself:

- *Have I truly observed the rhythm of my workplace?*
- *Do I understand what's valued here, or am I assuming?*
- *Am I blending in just to survive, or adapting to thrive?*

This is your chance to step back and check in, not just with your role, but with how you are showing up.

Grab your favourite journal, crack your knuckles, or type into that Notes app like you are writing a viral caption. Let's take a moment to align your inner compass with the culture around you.

Because thriving in any workplace starts with understanding yourself within it.

Self-Evaluation Activity

THE CULTURE COMPASS

Why does this activity matter?

This exercise helps you navigate the complexities of corporate culture and find a balance between fitting in and staying true to yourself.

By understanding and adapting to your organization's culture, you will be better equipped to thrive in your career and build positive relationships with your colleagues.

Ready to dive in?

Step	What to do?	Respond to your questions.
Observe the Culture	Spend a week observing the culture of your workplace. Pay attention to: • Communication style: Is it formal or informal? Direct or indirect? • Decision-making: Is it top-down or collaborative? • Values: What does the organization prioritize (innovation, customer focus, teamwork)? • Norms: What are the written/unwritten rules (dress code, working hours, meeting etiquette)?	
Identify Cultural Fit and Gaps	Think about how well you fit into the culture. Write down: • What aspects of the culture align with your values and work style? • What aspects feel challenging or uncomfortable? • Are there any gaps between your behaviour and the cultural expectations?	
Create an Adaptation Plan	Based on your observations, write down 2-3 actionable steps to adapt to the culture. For example: • If the culture values collaboration, make an effort to participate in team activities and build relationships.	

	• If the culture is more formal, adjust your communication style to be more professional. • If the culture prioritizes innovation, look for opportunities to share new ideas and take calculated risks.	
Seek Feedback	Ask a trusted colleague or mentor for feedback on how well you are adapting to the culture. For example: • *"Do you think I am aligning well with the team's communication style?"* • *"Is there anything I could do differently to fit in better?"*	
Reflect and Adjust	After a month, revisit your adaptation plan and reflect: • How well have you adapted to the culture? • Are there any new observations or challenges? • What adjustments do you need to make moving forward?	

Okay fam, real talk.

Corporate culture? It's kind of like a group chat. Sometimes it's vibing with memes, teamwork, and Friday fun. Sometimes it's all dry texts, weird rules, and that one person who keeps "replying all."

But here's the truth: you've got options.

You can adapt. You can lead. You can vibe high, or you can vibe out. The point is, you don't have to shrink yourself to fit in. Instead, learn the codes, understand the game, and then decide how you want to play.

Maybe you will be the one who sparks more openness. Maybe you will lead by example and bring in better energy. Or maybe you will say, "*Nope, not my people*," and respectfully peace out to a place that aligns better.

The choice is always yours. You are not stuck. You are just learning the map so you can either navigate it or redesign it. And hey, speaking of adapting, I didn't grow up texting in emojis or using "mood" as a full sentence, but look at me now. I met you where you are, because that's what adapting to a new culture looks like. I flexed my style to speak your language, and maybe that's the most underrated leadership skill of all.

So, take that energy forward. Read the room. Understand the vibes. And then? Decide if you want to blend in, stand out, or build something better. You've got this. In the world of hashtags, #ThrivingNotJustSurviving

Leverage Birbal's Wisdom in Action
Ahem. Imagine me, Birbal, the original corporate whisperer of the Mughal Empire, pulling up a beanbag in your breakout zone, *chai* in hand, hoodie on point.
Listen up, young hustlers. Back in the day, I didn't have Teams chat or office memes (*though I did have my fair share of royal tea*), but I learnt one timeless truth:
You don't win the game by shouting the loudest. You win by knowing when to speak, when to listen, and when to play your move.
In Akbar's court, everyone had their own vibe, some flexed power, some played politics, and some just tried to survive. But me? I observed. I adapted. I didn't fake it. I just figured out how to stay true to my brainy, cheeky self while navigating the chaos like a pro.
And guess what? That's your move too. Watch the flow.
• Understand the game. • Don't lose yourself trying to fit in, but know when to blend in to build trust.

> - And then? Use that trust to lead, shift the vibe, or rewrite the script.
>
> Being culturally smart isn't selling out. It's showing up with emotional intelligence, knowing which battles to pick, and thriving without burning out. So whether your manager is a boomer who still prints emails, or a millennial who ends every message with ":)" ... or you are just trying to decode meeting room politics, channel your inner Birbal.
>
> Adapt. Align. And then, shine.
>
> Your vibe, with a little wisdom, is the ultimate power move.

One quote that has always stayed with me, especially during times when I struggled to find my place or adapt to new environments, is by Peter Drucker, the father of modern management.

This quote has been a game-changer for me. No matter how brilliant your ideas are, how sharp your skills, or how ambitious your goals, if you don't understand the culture you are in, it's like running a race in the wrong direction. I have learnt (*sometimes the hard way*) that adapting to the culture isn't about losing who you are, it's about learning the terrain, playing smart, and growing stronger with every step.

As you step into different organizations, teams, and roles, carry this wisdom with you. Observe, absorb, adapt, and then, lead the culture forward when it's your turn.

"CULTURE EATS STRATEGY FOR BREAKFAST."
— PETER DRUCKER

CHAPTER 10

YOUR CREDIBILITY SPEAKS
LET YOUR ACTIONS DEFINE YOU

Let's talk about something in the corporate world that's rarer than a full inbox with zero unread emails. Yep, that quiet little superpower that doesn't shout, but definitely speaks volumes.

CREDIBILITY

Meet Aanya. A fresh graduate with a spark in her eyes, a killer résumé, and a dream to make it big in the corporate world. On her first day, she was enthusiastic, dressed sharp, and ready to conquer meetings like a boss. But as weeks went by, Aanya noticed something curious.

She wasn't getting looped into important conversations. Her suggestions in team meetings were acknowledged but rarely acted upon. And even though she worked late and gave her best, something was missing.

Then one day, her mentor gently said, *"Aanya, people don't trust words here, they trust patterns."*

That hit her hard.

So she stepped back and observed. She noticed the colleague who everyone leaned on, not because he was the loudest in the room, but because he delivered every single time. She saw how another team member never missed a deadline and always owned up when she messed up. They didn't do anything dramatic. They were just... consistent.

Aanya realized something crucial: credibility isn't built in a day, it's built in the quiet, everyday moments when no one's watching but everyone's noticing.

She began focusing on the small things, replying on time, keeping her promises, not overcommitting, and asking for help when needed. Slowly but surely, trust began to grow. Her manager began to depend on her. Her teammates looped her in early. Her voice began to carry weight.

Because here's the secret:

Credibility isn't about being the loudest. It's about being the most trusted.

It's not built by big wins, it's built by small, consistent actions.

And once you earn it? It'll take you further than any certification ever will.

So ask yourself, *are you becoming someone people can count on?*

Let's unpack what that really means.

Let's Learn from Birbal's Life Event

Long ago, in the dazzling court of Emperor Akbar, trust was rare and power was fickle. Whispers and flattery often filled the royal halls, and courtiers did what they had to, just to stay in favour. But among them stood one man who played a different game (*we all know him very well)*, Birbal.

He wasn't the richest. He didn't wear the fanciest robes. He didn't even try to impress Akbar with grand gestures. But what he did have was, credibility; earned not through words, but through consistent actions, sharp wisdom, and doing the right thing even when no one was watching.

One day, a theft occurred in the royal treasury. Gold coins meant for building shelters had disappeared overnight. Suspicion ran wild, and every minister began looking over their shoulder. Akbar was furious. *"I want the thief found, but no one shall be punished without proof,"* he declared.

Many tried to solve the case, but only Birbal stepped forward with confidence.

"Your Majesty" Birbal said, *"Allow me to catch the culprit. But I will need one thing: a room, and a magical lamp."*

"A magical lamp?" Akbar raised an eyebrow.

Birbal smiled. *"Yes. A lamp that only responds to truth."*

Intrigued, Akbar allowed it.

That night, Birbal gathered all the ministers and guards suspected in the case into a chamber. In the centre stood a large, covered lamp.

"This," Birbal declared dramatically, *"is the Lamp of Truth. It glows slightly brighter if touched by someone who is innocent. But for those who are guilty, it stays dim."*

One by one, he asked them to step in alone and touch the lamp.

The next morning, Birbal addressed the court.

"I have found your thief."

He turned to one of the ministers and pointed, *"It is him."*

The minister's face turned pale. *"How can you say that? There is no proof!"*

Birbal calmly pulled off the cloth covering the lamp.

It was just an ordinary lamp.

"You see," Birbal said, *"the lamp was coated with fine black soot. I asked everyone to touch it in the dark. When we turned the lights on, everyone's hands were black, except his. Because he never touched the lamp. He feared it would expose him."*

Akbar let out a hearty laugh. *"Brilliant!"*

Everyone gasped at the simplicity and cleverness, of the act.

But Akbar saw more. *"You didn't just solve the mystery, Birbal. You showed me why you are the only one I trust without question."*

Birbal didn't need titles or theatrics. He built credibility by:

- Being consistent with his words and actions
- Acting with integrity, even when the pressure was high
- Thinking creatively, without compromising on truth
- Standing for justice, not popularity

His credibility didn't just help him solve problems, it gave him lasting influence and trust in the emperor's eyes. He became the voice Akbar listened to, even when others spoke louder.

In today's corporate corridors, you might not have a magical lamp, but you do have your word, your follow-through, and your integrity. That's your real power.

People may forget your PowerPoint slides, but they will always remember if they could trust you when it mattered.

So ask yourself:

Do your actions match your promises?

Can people rely on you without double-checking?

Are you building your brand through trust or theatrics?

Just like Birbal, you don't need to be the flashiest in the room. Be the most reliable. Because in the long run, credibility always outshines charisma.

Here are your learnings.

1. **Credibility is the new currency**
   It's what makes people trust and respect you.

Imagine you are playing a long-term strategy game, like building your own empire in Minecraft or levelling up in a role-playing game. You collect resources, earn trust with your tribe, and build alliances. But there's one thing that unlocks the real boss levels in the corporate world - credibility.

In the workplace, credibility is like that ultra-rare power-up that doesn't just help you win once, it keeps unlocking new levels of influence, trust, and opportunity.

And here's the real deal: Credibility isn't gifted. It's earned, through your actions, your integrity, and your consistency. People don't trust you just because you say the right things. They trust you because you have shown up, followed through, and kept it real, even when things got tough, boring, or chaotic.

Think about that one teammate who always delivers before the deadline. Or the leader who owns their mistakes instead of blaming the team. Or the colleague who doesn't chase applause but earns respect by doing the right thing, day after day.

That's credibility in action.

It's not about being perfect. It's about being reliable. It's about making your actions so solid that your name carries weight even when you are not in the room.

In today's world, where everyone's talking, tweeting, and posting, credibility is what actually speaks for you.

- Be consistent - Let your results speak louder than your emails.
- Be dependable - If you say you will do it, actually do it.
- Be honest - Especially when it's hard. That's when credibility grows.
- Be kind - Because respect isn't just earned through knowledge, but through emotional intelligence.

Credibility might not trend on your feed, but trust us, it will trend in the minds of people who matter.

2. Actions Speak Louder Than Words, Like, Way Louder

Let's be real for a second.

Anyone can say, "*I am reliable.*"

But can they prove it without using a single word? That's where the real magic of credibility lies.

In a world filled with captions, bios, and beautifully crafted "I-am-so-productive" LinkedIn updates, it's not what you say, it's what you consistently do that earns respect.

Think of it like this:

You wouldn't trust a food delivery app that says your order is on the way. but it never shows up.

You wouldn't believe someone who claims to be a team player but disappears every time there's actual work.

See the pattern?

- *Your actions are your personal brand.*
- *Your consistency is the logo.*
- *And your behaviour? That's your tagline, clear, visible, and unforgettable.*

Want to be taken seriously? Don't just talk the talk, walk it, jog it, and sometimes even run it when needed.

Missed a deadline? Own it.

Promised a follow-up? Send it.

Said you would support a colleague? Show up.

Because credibility isn't built in the moments you speak, it's built in the moments you show up without needing to.

People won't always remember what you said, but they will remember how you behaved.

Here's something they don't always tell you during on-boarding or in college workshops.

Credibility isn't an overnight delivery.

It's not an Amazon Prime package. It's more like a slow-cooked, home-style biryani, layered with trust, time, and a whole lot of consistency.

Think about it.

You can't just walk into a new job and expect everyone to trust you right away. Credibility is earned, not given. It's built quietly, over time, through everyday moments.

Showing up when you say you will.
Following through on commitments, even the small ones.
Owning up when you mess up.
Staying true to your word, especially when no one's watching.

And yes, it takes time - weeks, months, even years, but that's what makes it so powerful.

So, before we jump into this self-evaluation, take a deep breath and ask yourself:

Am I willing to invest in becoming someone people trust?

Because once you have got credibility, doors open, voices listen, and opportunities find you.

Let's figure out where you stand and how you can grow from here. Ready? Let's go.

Self-Evaluation Activity

THE CREDIBILITY CHECKLIST

Why does this activity matter?

This exercise helps you take control of your credibility and ensure it aligns with your goals and values.

By being intentional about your actions and behaviour, you can build a reputation that earns trust and respect. Remember, your credibility is your professional legacy, make it count.

This is the last chapter with a Self-Evaluation Activity, make the most out of it.

Step	What to do?	Respond to your questions.
Reflect on Your Credibility	Think about your current level of credibility. Ask yourself: • *Do I consistently deliver on my promises?* • *Do I communicate clearly and honestly?* • *Do my actions align with my values and the organization's values?*	
Identify Areas for Improvement	Based on your reflections, identify specific areas where you can improve your credibility. For example: • If you sometimes miss deadlines, focus on improving your time management. • If you struggle with clear communication, practice active listening and be more concise in your messages. • If you have made mistakes in the past, take responsibility and make amends.	
Create a Credibility Action Plan	Write down 2-3 actionable steps to strengthen your credibility. For example: • *"I will always meet deadlines by setting realistic goals and prioritizing tasks."*	

	• *"I will communicate more clearly by preparing for meetings and following up with summaries."* • *"I will align my actions with my values by being honest and transparent in all my interactions."*	
Seek Feedback	Ask a trusted colleague or mentor for feedback on your credibility. For example: • *"Do you think I am reliable and consistent in my work?"* • *"Is there anything I could do differently to build more trust with the team?"*	
Monitor Your Progress	After a month, revisit your credibility action plan and reflect: • Have you noticed any changes in how others perceive you? • Are there any new areas for improvement? • What can you do to continue building your credibility?	

Here's something you really need to hear:

You are being watched. Every single time!

And no, not in a creepy Big Brother kind of way, more like in a "people-are-always-observing-how-you-show-up" kind of way.

Think about it.

Ever sneezed in a meeting and someone said, *"Bless you"*?

Yep, people notice the little things. So if they catch that, you better believe they are noticing whether you meet deadlines, support your teammates, or roll your eyes when someone's speaking *(I have been caught in the act more times than I'd like to admit, especially those perfectly timed eye rolls (yep, guilty!). Let's just say I have learnt the hard way that it's best to save the drama for when I am home and talking to my dog.).*

That's the reality of the workplace, your credibility is being built or broken every single day, through tiny, seemingly invisible moments.

Here's your big takeaway:

- Don't just preach it. Practice it.
- Let your actions be so aligned with your values that people trust you without question.
- Let your name be a brand that silently says: *"I deliver. I care. I'm solid."*

You are your own billboard, so ask yourself,

What's the message you are broadcasting?

Because your credibility? That's your golden badge in the corporate world.

Make sure it shines.

Leverage Birbal's Wisdom in Action

If Birbal were sliding into your Zoom meeting today, here's what he would probably say:

"Dear Young Mind, in Akbar's court, I didn't earn trust by being the loudest voice, I earned it by being the most reliable one.

I showed up with facts, solutions, and the occasional punchline, but I never showed off. People trusted me not because I spoke well, but because my actions did the talking. That's how I became irreplaceable."

The moral?

> Credibility isn't gifted, it's built, brick by brick, with consistency, courage, and character.
>
> One misstep can shake it, but a lifetime of good choices can anchor it like bedrock.
>
> So be like Birbal, walk the talk, lead with integrity, and if you ever doubt yourself, ask: *Would Birbal roll his eyes in court, or would he raise a clever brow and deliver the truth with class?*
>
> Your credibility is your crown. Wear it wisely, polish it often, and never trade it for shortcuts.

As we wrap up this chapter on credibility, I want to leave you with a quote that has been my anchor during the most defining moments of my career.

Every time I faced a tough call, a tempting shortcut, or an uncomfortable truth, I reminded myself that I am building something far bigger than a moment: I am building a life, a legacy. And so are you.

You always have a choice. You can choose shortcuts, or you can choose values. You can let the noise shape you, or you can let your integrity guide you. You can build a reputation that glows even when no one is watching. The pen is in your hand. You are the author. So go ahead, build the kind of life you would be proud to sign your name to.

> "IT TAKES 20 YEARS TO BUILD A REPUTATION AND FIVE MINUTES TO RUIN IT. IF YOU THINK ABOUT THAT, YOU'LL DO THINGS DIFFERENTLY."
> — WARREN BUFFETT

CHAPTER 11

FREQUENTLY USED CORPORATE JARGONS

Speak the Lingo - Cracking the Corporate Code

You have made it this far, and that means you are already better equipped than most fresh entrants to the corporate jungle. But before we close this book, let's talk about one of the most underrated tools in your corporate toolkit.

LANGUAGE

You know, those buzzwords and phrases that people throw around in meetings, emails, and presentations. Phrases like "circle back," "low-hanging fruit," and "synergy" might sound impressive, or intimidating, at first, but let's be real: they can also feel like an entirely new dialect if you are just starting out.

Here's the thing, corporate lingo isn't just for sounding smart or "fitting in." It's a way professionals communicate quickly and efficiently. But if you would not know, you might find yourself nodding through meetings wondering if you accidentally walked into a foreign film without subtitles.

Don't worry, you are not alone. We have all been there. And the good news is, once you start learning these terms, you won't just understand the conversations, you will be able to lead them.

So think of the next section as your Corporate Dictionary - Unfiltered Edition. It's not just definitions; it's context, meaning, and strategy all rolled into one. Consider this your cheat sheet to sounding savvy, decoding signals, and making sense of those oddly motivational phrases floating around the office.

FREQUENTLY USED CORPORATE JARGONS

And hey, knowing this lingo won't just make you look good, it will help you connect, contribute, and climb.

Here is your Corporate Lingo Cheat Sheet: Decode Like a Pro.

Corporate Jargon	What It Really Means?
Action items	Tasks that need to be completed after a meeting or discussion.
Bandwidth	Your ability or capacity to take on more work.
Boil the ocean	Trying to do too much at once - often unrealistic or overly ambitious.
Buy-in	Getting others' agreement or support to move forward.
Circle back	Let's revisit this topic later (or sometimes... never).
Close the loop	Finalizing an issue by confirming or reporting back.
Compliance	Following legal rules and company policies.
Core competencies	Key skills or strengths that define a team or role.
Credibility capital	The trust you earn by consistently delivering quality work.
Cultural fit	How well someone aligns with company values and team vibe.
DEI	Diversity, Equity, and Inclusion - important for fair and inclusive workplaces.
Deep dive	A thorough and detailed examination of a topic or problem.
Digital footprint	Your online reputation and how you appear professionally.
Do the right thing	Choose what's ethically correct, even when difficult.
Due diligence	Doing your homework before making a decision or commitment.

FREQUENTLY USED CORPORATE JARGONS

Elevator pitch	A quick and compelling summary of who you are and what you do.
Executive presence	Carrying yourself with confidence, poise, and credibility.
Flight risk	An employee who may be planning to leave the company.
Going above and beyond	Doing more than what's required or expected.
Holistic approach	Considering the full picture, not just individual parts.
Hit the ground running	Start a new task or role quickly and effectively.
Invisible workload	Behind-the-scenes work that's necessary but often unrecognized.
It's not a good fit	A polite way to reject someone or something.
Let's park this	Put this idea aside for now; we may or may not revisit it later.
Low-hanging fruit	The easiest opportunities or tasks that bring quick results.
Manage up	Proactively and smartly working with your manager to align and succeed.
Move the needle	Make a real, measurable impact.
Non-negotiables	Values or standards you won't compromise on.
Open-door policy	A management style where leaders are approachable and open to feedback.
Pain point	A recurring problem or challenge that needs to be addressed.
Perception is reality	How people see you becomes the truth in their minds.
Pivot	Quickly changing strategy or approach.
Personal brand	The unique impression others have of you at work.
Process adherence	Sticking to approved processes and protocols.

Promotion readiness	Being seen as capable and prepared for the next role.
Reputation management	Actively shaping and protecting your professional image.
Run it up the flagpole	Test an idea to see how others react before making it official.
Seamless experience	A smooth and trouble-free journey for the end-user or team.
Shout-out	A public thank-you or recognition for someone's work.
Stakeholder alignment	Making sure all decision-makers agree and are on the same page.
Strategic alignment	Ensuring that work supports the company's broader goals.
Succession planning	Preparing someone to take over a key role in the future.
Synergy	When two people or teams produce better results together than apart.
Take this offline	Let's discuss this outside of the current meeting or conversation.
Think outside the box	Be creative, unconventional, and explore new ideas.
Thought leader	Someone known for innovative, respected thinking in their field.
Touch base	Check in briefly with someone to discuss updates or progress.
Track record	Your past performance and reliability over time.
Trust but verify	Give people the benefit of the doubt, but still confirm.
Value-add	Extra benefits or contributions you bring to a project.
Visibility matters	Being seen and noticed at work helps build influence and recognition.

FREQUENTLY USED CORPORATE JARGONS

Walk the talk	Align your actions with your words and promises.
Watercooler talk	Casual office conversations, often gossip or informal updates.
Win-win	A solution where everyone benefits.

Go ahead, speak the language. Be heard. Be understood. And most importantly, be you, but the most well-informed version of you possible.

ACKNOWLEDGEMENTS & REFERENCES

The Akbar-Birbal stories woven throughout this book are inspired by a rich tradition of Indian folk tales that have been shared orally for centuries. These timeless stories of wit, wisdom, and cleverness have transcended generations. While no single original author can be credited, their enduring legacy continues to offer valuable lessons that resonate, even in today's fast-paced corporate world.

Many versions of these stories have been published in children's books, anthologies, and digital platforms. Some well-known storytellers and authors have beautifully retold these tales, adding their unique voice and perspective. I have adapted these folk tales in my own words to make them relatable and relevant for Generation Z and Alpha entering the corporate landscape.

The analogies and lessons drawn from Birbal's life are inspired by this collective heritage of storytelling, blended with contemporary insights from leadership and workplace culture.

I extend my gratitude to all the storytellers, authors, and creators, past and present, who have kept the spirit of Akbar and Birbal alive through their creativity and dedication. This book stands on the shoulders of these timeless narratives and reflects an ongoing journey of learning and adaptation in the corporate world.

Lastly, to you, my reader:

Whether you're a fresher just stepping into your first office or someone still finding their way through the cubicles and conversations, I thank you. You inspire me to blend tradition with today's realities, and to write with integrity, humour, and courage.

I have a special message for you.

Flip to the next page to read it.

AUTHOR'S LETTER FOR YOU!

My dearest reader,

Yes, you, the dreamer standing at the threshold of the corporate world with a spark in your eyes and maybe a few butterflies in your stomach. I see you.

And I want you to know something very important: you are not alone.

Not now. Not ever.

As you step into this vast, competitive, and sometimes chaotic world, it might feel overwhelming. There will be days filled with joy and others with confusion. Moments of self-doubt, and others when you will surprise even yourself. Through it all, remember, you are not walking this path solo.

Your parents, teachers, well-wishers, friends, mentors, and I are all right here. Standing by your side, silently rooting for you, clapping loudly for your wins (big and small), and sending you strength when things get tough. We are your invisible cheer squad, and you can always reach out when you need someone to talk to.

If you ever feel lost, unsure, or just want to share how your journey is unfolding, email me at sangeeta16mukherji@gmail.com

We can hop on a quick call, have a heart-to-heart, or simply share a laugh. Sometimes, that's all it takes to feel lighter.

Also, I would love to hear what this book did for you.

Did it help?

If yes, what touched you the most? If not, then tell me, why not?

Your feedback means everything to me, because your journey matters.

AUTHOR'S LETTER FOR YOU!

You have every right to dream big, grow strong, fall, rise, and shine in your own beautiful way. Don't rush the process. Don't chase perfection. Just be you, curious, kind, bold, and ready to learn.

Because the world doesn't need another perfect employee.

It needs you, your story, your ideas, your spark.

And here's one life mantra I live by:

Life is simple. Don't complicate it. And most importantly, have fun all the way

With all my love and belief in you,

Sangeeta Mukherjee

Your forever cheerleader

www.ingramcontent.com/pod-product-compliance
Lightning Source LLC
LaVergne TN
LVHW041853070526
838199LV00045BB/1581